Everyday Easy Vegan

90 fuss-free recipes,
six weeks of meal plans
all pure plant-based

Faye James

CONTENTS

Please Note: Weights, measures, temperatures, conversions and nutritional analyses are approximate and subject to individual variation for convenience, because we are using natural ingredients and allowing for variations in equipment.

When buying cans, get the nearest equivalent sizes as available in your area.

Please Note: Some recipes might contain potential allergens or trigger food sensitivities. Please consult with your doctor or a qualified nutritionist if in doubt.

About the Author

Faye James is a leading voice in nutrition, wellness, and women's health, with over 20 years of experience helping individuals live more vibrant, balanced lives through the power of food. As an Accredited Nutritionist and a member of both the Nutrition Council Australia and the Australian Menopause Society, Faye blends expert knowledge with a deeply practical, real-world approach to healthy living.

She is the bestselling author of *The Perimenopause Plan* (2025) *The Menopause Diet* (2023), *The 10:10 Diet* (2019), and *The Long Life Plan* (2018), and her passion lies in simplifying science-backed wellness so it fits into even the busiest lifestyles. Her recipes, advice, and programs have supported thousands of women to boost energy, improve digestion, balance hormones, and feel empowered in their food choices.

Faye's writing has been featured in top publications including *ELLE*, *Body+Soul*, *Women's Health*, *Prevention*, *Glamour*, *Harper's Bazaar* and *HELLO!*. She has also collaborated with major health and lifestyle brands like Woolworths, Weight Watchers, Fitness First, and Goodlife Health Clubs, providing expert insights on everything from meal planning to mindful eating.

In *Everyday Easy Vegan*, Faye brings her trademark warmth and expertise to the world of plant-based eating. With over 90 simple, delicious recipes and six weeks of structured meal plans and shopping lists, the book is a practical and inspiring guide to making plant-based meals feel easy, achievable, and full of joy.

Originally from London and now based in Sydney, Faye lives with her husband – food photographer Darrin James – and their two teen children. Passionate about using food as medicine, she continues to dedicate her career to helping others feel their best, one nourishing meal at a time.

Welcome to Easy Vegan

Hi there,

I'm Faye James, a nutritionist, recipe developer, health journalist, mother, and passionate advocate for feeling your best through the power of good food. I created *Everyday Easy Vegan* to make plant-based eating simpler, more approachable and more joyful. This isn't about strict rules or perfection. It's about adding more colour, flavour and nourishment to your plate in a way that fits your life.

Whether you're trying out Meat-Free Mondays, already plant-based, or simply curious about eating more mindfully, this book is here to support you. Inside, you'll find over 100 easy, fuss-free, vegan recipes, plus six weeks of meal plans and shopping lists to make everyday cooking less of a juggle.

Before we get into the food, I wanted to share a little background, the science, the common myths, and the small shifts that can make this lifestyle not just doable but deeply rewarding. Because when we feel informed and inspired, healthy choices become second nature.

Why Choose Vegan – The Real Benefits

Choosing to follow a vegan lifestyle isn't just about what's on your plate, it's about how those daily choices ripple outwards to influence your overall well being, the environment, and even your connection with the world around you.

It's about feeling energised and aligned with your values, whatever they may be. I've seen it time and time again in clients, once they shift towards a more plant-based way of eating, their energy improves, digestion settles, their skin clears, and there's a kind of lightness that returns. People often describe feeling more mentally focused and emotionally steady. Some even tell me they feel more in tune with themselves, as if they've finally found a way of eating that feels natural, nourishing and right for their body.

For many, aches and pains start to subside, hormonal fluctuations begin to even out, and that constant bloated, heavy feeling starts to lift. Some notice fewer colds and infections throughout the year, better recovery after exercise, and even improved sleep quality. And then there's the unexpected bonus, a renewed sense of creativity in the kitchen. When you start building meals around plants, you're suddenly playing with colour, texture, and global flavours in a way that feels exciting rather than restrictive.

The EPIC-Oxford study, which followed more than 65,000 people in the UK, found that vegans had a 32% lower risk of heart disease than meat-eaters. That's a pretty powerful stat. And a 2021 review published in *PLOS Medicine* found that diets rich in whole plant foods also significantly lowered the risk of type 2 diabetes.

So, what's behind these benefits?

Plants are naturally high in fibre, antioxidants, and a range of vitamins and minerals – and lower in saturated fat and cholesterol. This combination helps calm inflammation, support immunity, balance blood sugar and improve digestion.

There's also growing research showing that plant-based diets can support mental health. The fibre in plant foods feeds beneficial gut bacteria, which are directly involved in producing mood-regulating neurotransmitters like serotonin. That gut-brain connection is powerful, and nourishing it with whole foods may help reduce symptoms of anxiety and depression.

Skin health is another big one. It's not uncommon to see improvements within just a few weeks, especially when processed foods are swapped for whole, nutrient-dense ingredients. Vegan diets tend to naturally reduce inflammatory triggers and increase antioxidants like vitamin C, beta carotene and selenium, all of which support tissue repair and collagen production. As a nutritionist, it's always lovely to hear someone say their skin is glowing, or they're waking up feeling fresher than they have in years.

And there's the bigger picture too. When we zoom out and look beyond personal health, there's a huge positive impact on our environment, too. Research published in *Science* (Poore & Nemecek, 2018) suggests that going vegan is one of the most impactful things we can do for the planet. It can cut greenhouse gas emissions, water usage, and land use, all in one simple dietary shift.

So, whether you're motivated by health, the environment, animal welfare, or all of the above, embracing a more plant-based way of eating is an empowering step. It's a shift that not only supports your health, but helps create a kinder and more sustainable world. And it doesn't have to be all or nothing, even small changes can have a big impact over time.

Going Plant-Based for Menopausal Women

Navigating menopause is a deeply personal experience, and nutrition can be one of your most supportive tools along the way. A plant-based diet, rich in whole foods, offers numerous benefits that can help ease some of the most common menopausal challenges, from hot flushes and disrupted sleep to weight gain and mood swings.

Alleviating Hot Flushes and Night Sweats

Hot flushes and night sweats are among the most frequently reported menopausal symptoms. Research, including the Women's Study for the Alleviation of Vasomotor Symptoms (WAVS), has shown that following a low-fat, plant-based diet enriched with soy can lead to a significant reduction in these symptoms. In fact, participants in the study experienced an 84% decrease in moderate-to-severe hot flushes over 12 weeks, without the use of hormone therapy.

Supporting Hormonal Balance with Phytoestrogens

Phytoestrogens are naturally occurring compounds found in plant foods like soybeans, flaxseeds and legumes. These compounds can mimic oestrogen in the body and may help to balance hormone levels. For many women, including more of these foods in their diet has been shown to help with mood swings, irritability and other emotional symptoms linked to hormonal changes.

Strengthening Bone Health

After menopause, the drop in oestrogen increases the risk of bone loss. A well-planned plant-based diet can provide key nutrients for bone support – including calcium, magnesium, and vitamin K – found in foods like leafy greens, tofu, almonds and calcium-fortified plant milks.

Supporting Heart Health

Heart health becomes more important after menopause, as oestrogen's protective effect begins to decline. Plant-based diets are naturally lower in saturated fat and cholesterol and have been associated with lower blood pressure and improved cholesterol levels. Regularly including whole grains, pulses, fruits and vegetables can help reduce the risk of cardiovascular disease.

Supporting Weight and Metabolism

Many women find it harder to manage their weight during menopause. Plant-based diets are high in fibre and lower in calorie density, which means they can help you feel full and satisfied without overeating. The WAVS study also noted that participants lost an average of eight pounds over 12 weeks on a plant-based diet, even without focusing on weight loss.

The Protein Myth: Getting Enough on a Vegan Diet

If I had a dollar for every time someone asked, "But where do you get your protein?" – I could probably open my own tofu factory.

The truth is, all whole plant foods contain

protein. And when you eat a mix of them throughout the day – legumes, whole grains, nuts, seeds and vegetables – you'll easily meet your needs.

The general recommendation is 0.8 g of protein per kilogram (0.2 oz per stone) of body weight for the average adult. So if you weigh 70 kg (11 stone), that's about 56 g (2 oz) a day. And yes, you can absolutely hit that on a plant-based diet without needing powders or protein bars.

Here's what that might look like in real food:

- 1 cup cooked lentils = 18 g (0.6 oz) protein
- 100 g tofu = 14 g (0.5 oz) protein
- 1 cup cooked quinoa = 8 g (0.3 oz) protein
- 2 tbsp peanut butter = 8 g (0.3 oz) protein
- 1 cup cooked chickpeas = 15 g (0.53 oz) protein

Even if you're very active, pregnant or breastfeeding, with a little planning and variety, plant protein can more than keep up.

It's also worth noting that while some plant foods don't contain all nine essential amino acids on their own, your body is great at pulling what it needs from different meals throughout the day. You don't need to worry about "complete" proteins in every bite – just eat a range of whole foods and your body will take care of the rest.

The Academy of Nutrition and Dietetics agrees that well-planned vegan diets are suitable for all life stages, including childhood, pregnancy and athletic performance.

Why Plant Protein is a Game Changer

Beyond just being enough, plant protein offers a whole lot more. Unlike animal protein, plant-based sources are naturally free from cholesterol and often lower in saturated fat. They're also typically rich in fibre and come with powerful antioxidants that support overall health.

Here are a few of my favourites:

- **Tofu and tempeh**: Great sources of calcium and iron. They're also rich in isoflavones, which may support hormonal balance and bone health.
- **Lentils and chickpeas**: Affordable, versatile, and packed with fibre, protein and iron.
- **Chia, flax and hemp seeds**: Excellent sources of omega-3s and magnesium, which can support mood and reduce inflammation.
- **Quinoa**: A complete protein that's also rich in B vitamins, magnesium and iron.

Plus, when you start eating more plant protein, you naturally end up eating more colour and variety. From hearty grain bowls to fragrant curries and fresh salads, the options are endless – and your gut (and taste buds) will thank you for it.

Common Pitfalls on a Plant-Based Diet

While eating plant-based can be incredibly nourishing, there are a few key nutrients to be mindful of. The good news? With a little awareness, they're all easy to stay on top of.

Vitamin B12

This one's important. B12 is essential for nerve health and red blood cell production, but it's not naturally found in plant foods. That's why I recommend taking a supplement or choosing fortified foods like nutritional yeast or plant-based milks.

Iron and Zinc

Plant-based iron (called non-heme iron) isn't absorbed quite as efficiently as the iron found in animal products. But there's an easy fix: eat it with a source of vitamin C (like citrus, tomatoes or capsicum) to help boost absorption.

Try to avoid tea and coffee with meals as the tannins can block iron uptake.

Calcium and Vitamin D

You can get plenty of calcium on a vegan diet from tofu, tahini, leafy greens and fortified plant milks. Just keep an eye on your daily intake. Vitamin D is a little harder to get from food, especially in winter – so a supplement may be a smart option.

Omega-3s

These essential fats help with brain health, mood, and inflammation. Chia, flax and walnuts are great, but to get enough EPA and DHA (the most active forms), you might want to consider an algae oil supplement.

Processed Vegan Foods

There are so many amazing plant-based convenience foods on the market right now – and I'm all for the occasional shortcut. But not all vegan products are created equal. Some are high in salt, sugar or oils. Try to keep the focus on whole, minimally processed foods as your foundation.

SIX-WEEK MEAL PLANS

From nourishing breakfasts to hearty dinners, comforting soups to indulgent desserts

WEEK 1 MEAL PLAN

DAY	BREAKFAST	LUNCH	SNACK	DINNER
Monday	Sweet Potato & Tofu Hash	Sweet Potato & Black Bean Quesadillas	Spiced Banana & Cinnamon Smoothie	Pumpkin & Red Lentil Soup
Tuesday	Sweet Potato & Tofu Hash	Zesty Turkish Couscous Salad	Spiced Banana & Cinnamon Smoothie	One-Pot Mustardy Chickpeas
Wednesday	White Bean & Tomato Stew	Zesty Turkish Couscous Salad	Spiced Banana & Cinnamon Smoothie	One-Pot Mustardy Chickpeas
Thursday	White Bean & Tomato Stew	Lemony Chickpea & Zucchini Salad	Caramel Coconut Cheesecake	Crispy Tofu in Tomato Sauce
Friday	Banana Bread Breakfast Oats	Lemony Chickpea & Zucchini Salad	Caramel Coconut Cheesecake	Crispy Tofu in Tomato Sauce
Saturday	Banana Bread Breakfast Oats	Parsnip, Apple & White Bean Soup	Caramel Coconut Cheesecake	Meal Out – Enjoy!
Sunday	Sweet Potato & Black Bean Quesadillas	Parsnip, Apple & White Bean Soup	Caramel Coconut Cheesecake	One-Pot Thyme Mushroom Skillet

SHOPPING LIST

PRODUCE

- 1 red apple
- 1 avocado
- 4 bananas
- 3 lemons
- 1 lime
- 5 onions
- 1 red onion
- 1 bunch spring onions
- 2 shallots
- 1 leek
- 2 bulbs garlic
- Root ginger
- 2 tomatoes
- 1 cucumber
- 1 red bell pepper
- 1 chilli pepper
- 3 zucchini (courgettes)
- 250 g (8 oz) chestnut mushrooms
- 100 g (3½ oz) shiitake mushrooms
- 500 g (1 lb) parsnips
- ½ head broccoli
- 750 g (1½ lb) sweet potatoes (approx 5)
- 1 kg (2 lb) pumpkin
- Chives
- Coriander (cilantro)
- Parsley
- Rosemary
- Thyme

PROTEIN

- 750 g (1½ lb) block firm tofu
- 500 g (1 lb) canned chickpeas
- 1 kg (2 lb) canned cannellini beans
- 300 g (10 oz) canned black beans
- Plant-based cheddar cheese
- Plant-based cream cheese
- Plant-based Greek yogurt
- Plant-based coconut yogurt

DRY GOODS

- Rolled oats
- Couscous
- Red lentils
- Chia seeds
- Spelt flour
- Sugar
- Coconut sugar
- 8 whole wheat tortillas
- Unsweetened oat milk
- Unsweetened almond milk
- Unsweetened coconut milk
- Pecan nuts
- Almonds
- 16 medjool dates
- 200 g (7 oz) pitted dates

STAPLES & MISC

- Ice cubes
- Plant-based butter
- Cornstarch (corn flour)
- Vanilla extract
- Black pepper
- Whole peppercorns
- Sweet paprika
- Chilli powder
- Red pepper flakes (chilli flakes)
- Pomegranate juice
- Ground cardamom
- Ground cumin
- Ground turmeric
- Salsa of choice
- Ground ginger
- Ground cinnamon
- Bay leaves
- Extra virgin olive oil
- Olive oil
- Sesame oil
- Maple syrup
- Tomato paste (tomato purée)
- 2 x 425 g (15 oz) cans chopped tomatoes
- Tahini
- Dijon mustard
- Soy sauce
- Vegetable stock (vegetable broth)
- Apple cider vinegar
- White balsamic vinegar
- White wine vinegar
- Sea salt
- Fine sea salt
- Plant-based cream

SERVES 2 | 10 MINUTES + OVERNIGHT

Banana Bread Breakfast Oats

INGREDIENTS

1 banana + extra ½ banana, sliced to garnish

100 g (3½ oz) rolled oats

200 ml (7 fl oz) plant based milk (oat milk)

30 g (1 oz) pecans, roughly chopped, divided

½ tsp ground cinnamon

1 tbsp maple syrup

60 g (2 oz) plant-based coconut yogurt

pinch of salt

METHOD

- Peel the whole banana and mash with a fork.
- Combine the mashed banana with rolled oats, oat milk, half of the pecans, cinnamon, maple syrup, and a pinch of salt.
- Transfer to jars with lids and refrigerate overnight.
- Before serving, garnish with coconut yogurt, banana slices and the remaining pecans.

Tip: Add a scoop of vegan protein powder to help reach your protein goals.

ENERGY	CARBS	PROTEIN	FAT
416 kcal (416 Cal)	60 g (2 oz)	8 g (0.3 oz)	16 g (0.6 oz)

SERVES 3 | 50 MINUTES

Sweet Potato & Tofu Hash

INGREDIENTS

1 red bell pepper, chopped

1 red onion, ¼ thinly sliced, remainder diced

1 sprig rosemary

425 g (15 oz) block firm tofu, cut into cubes

250 g (8 oz) sweet potato, cubed

2 tbsp cornstarch

2 ¼ tsp chilli powder, divided

3 tbsp olive oil

2 tsp & a 2 pinches of salt

1 tbsp apple cider vinegar

chopped parsley, to serve

METHOD

- Preheat the oven to 220°C (425°F). Line a sheet pan with baking paper.
- Toss the bell pepper, diced onion and rosemary with 1 tablespoon of olive oil, and a pinch of salt. Spread in a single layer on about a quarter of the sheet pan.
- In the same bowl, combine the tofu, sweet potato, cornstarch and 2 teaspoons of chilli powder.
- Season with 2 teaspoons of salt, toss with another 2 tablespoons of oil, then arrange in a single layer beside the peppers.
- Roast for 30–35 minutes until the vegetables are tender and the tofu is crisp.
- In a small bowl, combine the sliced onion with 1 tablespoon apple cider vinegar, remaining ¼ teaspoon of chilli powder and a pinch of salt. Serve with chopped parsley or Parsley Oil (page 21).

ENERGY	CARBS	PROTEIN	FAT
333 kcal (333 Cal)	21 g (0.7 oz)	15 g (0.5 oz)	21 g (0.7 oz)

SERVES 8 | 5 MINUTES

Parsley Oil

INGREDIENTS

8 tbsp olive oil

4 tbsp parsley, finely chopped

3 tsp white wine vinegar

pinch of fine sea salt

pinch of sugar

METHOD

- Stir all the ingredients together in a small bowl. Cover and refrigerate for up to 48 hours.

Tip: Add some garlic or lemon juice if you like a touch of pungency or acid.

ENERGY	CARBS	PROTEIN	FAT
126 kcal (126 Cal)	0 g (0 oz)	0 g (0 oz)	14 g (0.5 oz)

SERVES 6 | 1 HOUR 25 MINUTES

White Bean & Tomato Stew

INGREDIENTS

2 yellow onions, halved & sliced

200 g (7 oz) can chopped tomatoes, diced

4 cloves garlic, peeled & grated

3 tbsp parsley, finely chopped, plus extra to garnish

2 tsp sweet paprika

1 tsp ground ginger

1 tsp ground turmeric

500 ml (1 pt) vegetable stock

750 g (1½ lb) canned cannellini beans, drained

2 tbsp olive oil

1½ tsp salt

salt & pepper to taste

METHOD

- Place a large pot over medium-low heat, and warm 2 tablespoons of olive oil. Add the onions, cover the pot and sauté, stirring occasionally, for 7 minutes until soft.
- Add the diced tomatoes, garlic, parsley, paprika, ginger, turmeric and 1½ teaspoon of salt. Pour in vegetable stock, cover, and cook for 45 minutes.
- Now add the drained beans and cook for a further 20 minutes.
- Adjust seasoning to taste, serve with more chopped parsley or Parsley Oil (page 21).

ENERGY	CARBS	PROTEIN	FAT
208 kcal (208 Cal)	28 g (1.0 oz)	6 g (0.2 oz)	8 g (0.3 oz)

SERVES 2 | 30 MINUTES

Zesty Turkish Couscous Salad

INGREDIENTS

100 g (3½ oz) couscous

30 g (1 oz) tomato paste

15 g (½ oz) fresh parsley, chopped

3 green onions, finely sliced

1 lemon, ½ juiced, ½ cut into wedges for serving

¼ cucumber, finely diced

30 ml (1 fl oz) pomegranate juice

60 ml (2 fl oz) tomatoes, deseeded & finely diced

½ tsp ground cumin

100ml (3 fl oz) hot water

2 tbsp olive oil

salt for seasoning

METHOD

- Soak the couscous in 100 ml (3 fl oz) hot water for 20 minutes. While the couscous is soaking, prepare the vegetables.
- Combine the couscous with the remaining ingredients.
- Drizzle with 2 tablespoons of olive oil and season with salt, then mix well and serve with lemon wedges.

Tip: Add a cup of cooked chickpeas or lentils to increase protein intake.

ENERGY	CARBS	PROTEIN	FAT
367 kcal (367 Cal)	50 g (1.8 oz)	8 g (0.3 oz)	15 g (0.5 oz)

SERVES 2 | 30 MINUTES

Lemony Chickpea & Zucchini Salad

INGREDIENTS

3 zucchini (courgettes), spiralized into noodles

30 g (1 oz) tahini

1 lemon, juiced

2 tsp sesame oil

1 tbsp tamari

½ tsp red pepper flakes

250 g (8 oz) canned chickpeas, drained

½ shallot, finely diced

2 tbsp fresh parsley, chopped

salt & pepper to taste

water

METHOD

- Prepare the zucchini (courgettes) noodles using a spiralizer, or slice into ribbons with a vegetable peeler.
- In a small bowl, whisk together the tahini, lemon juice, sesame oil, tamari and red pepper flakes, thinning with water as needed. Adjust the seasoning with salt and pepper.
- In a large bowl, mix the zucchini noodles with the chickpeas, shallot, and dressing.
- Serve topped with additional sprinkle of red pepper flakes and parsley.

Tip: Don't like chickpeas? Cannellini beans also work well in this recipe too.

ENERGY	CARBS	PROTEIN	FAT
421 kcal (421 Cal)	49 g (1.7 oz)	18 g (0.6 oz)	17 g (0.6 oz)

SERVES 4 | 25 MINUTES

Sweet Potato & Black Bean Quesadillas

INGREDIENTS

125 g (4 oz) plant-based cheddar cheese, shredded

300 g (10 oz) sweet potato, cooked & mashed (about 2 small sweet potatoes)

300 g (10 oz) canned black beans, drained

8 whole-wheat tortillas

8 tbsp plant based Greek yogurt, to serve

1 avocado, sliced, to serve

8 tbsp salsa, to serve

METHOD

- In a medium bowl, mix together the shredded cheese, mashed sweet potato and black beans.
- Heat a large nonstick skillet over medium heat.
- Place one tortilla in the pan, warming for 20–30 seconds on each side until soft.
- Spread half of the cheese mixture over the tortilla, then top with a second tortilla.
- Press gently and cook until the bottom side is golden, about 1–2 minutes. Flip over and cook the other side for a further 2–3 minutes, until the cheese has melted.
- Repeat this process with remaining tortillas and filling.
- Slice and serve with yogurt, avocado and salsa.

ENERGY	CARBS	PROTEIN	FAT
566 kcal (566 Cal)	75 g (2.6 oz)	17 g (0.6 oz)	22 g (0.8 oz)

SERVES 4 | 30 MINUTES

Parsnip, Apple & White Bean Soup

INGREDIENTS

1 yellow onion, finely diced

425 g (15 oz) parsnips, peeled & diced

1 red apple, peeled, cored & diced

4 sprigs fresh thyme

1 clove garlic, minced

1L (2 pt) vegetable stock

250 g (8 oz) canned cannellini beans, drained

3 tbsp olive oil

salt

METHOD

- In a pot, heat 2 tablespoons of olive oil over medium-high heat.
- Add the onion and parsnips.
- Then sauté for 5 minutes until softened.
- Add the apple, thyme and garlic to the pot, cooking for a further 2 minutes.
- Pour in vegetable stock and cannellini beans, season with salt, then bring to a simmer and cook for 10 minutes.
- Blend the soup until smooth.
- Drizzle with 1 tablespoon of olive oil and serve.

ENERGY	CARBS	PROTEIN	FAT
319 kcal (319 Cal)	49 g (1.7 oz)	6 g (0.2 oz)	11 g (0.4 oz)

SERVES 2 | 30 MINUTES

One-Pot Mustardy Chickpeas

INGREDIENTS

1 leek, washed & sliced

2 cloves garlic, minced

250 ml (8 fl oz) vegetable stock

250 g (8 oz) canned chickpeas, reserve the brine

2 bay leaves

½ broccoli, cut into florets

½ tbsp Dijon mustard

½ lemon, juiced

15 g (½ oz) chives, chopped

2 tbsp olive oil

pinch of salt

METHOD

- Heat 2 tablespoons of olive oil in a pot over medium heat, and sauté the leeks and garlic with a pinch of salt for 10 minutes until softened.
- Add the vegetable stock, chickpeas and their brine, and bay leaves.
- Bring to a boil, then reduce heat to medium-low and simmer for 10 minutes.
- Remove the bay leaves, then puree ¼ of the mixture before returning it to the pot for a thicker consistency.
- Add the broccoli, cover the pot, and cook for a further 10 minutes.
- Stir in mustard and lemon juice, garnish with chives, and serve.

ENERGY	CARBS	PROTEIN	FAT
377 kcal (377 Cal)	43 g (1.5 oz)	13 g (0.5 oz)	17 g (0.6 oz)

SERVES 2 | 30 MINUTES

One-Pot Thyme Mushroom Skillet

INGREDIENTS

250 g (8 oz) button mushrooms, sliced

125 g (4 oz) shiitake mushrooms, sliced

1 yellow onion, finely diced

1 clove garlic, minced

4 sprigs thyme, leaves removed

100 ml (3 fl oz) plant based milk

200 ml (7 fl oz) plant-based cream

1 tbsp chopped parsley, to garnish

2 tbsp olive oil

1 tsp white balsamic vinegar

salt & pepper to taste

METHOD

- Heat 2 tablespoons of olive oil in a skillet, over medium heat.
- Add the mushrooms, onions and garlic and sauté for 3 minutes until fragrant.
- Add thyme leaves and continue to cook for 1 minute.
- Pour in the plant based milk and cream.
- Reduce the heat to low and simmer for 10 minutes.
- Add 1 teaspoon of white balsamic vinegar, season to taste with salt and pepper.
- Garnish with parsley and serve.

ENERGY	CARBS	PROTEIN	FAT
380 kcal (380 Cal)	26 g (0.9 oz)	6 g (0.2 oz)	28 g (1.0 oz)

SERVES 2 | 30 MINUTES

Crispy Tofu in Tomato Sauce

INGREDIENTS

300 g (10 oz) firm tofu, cut into triangles

1 shallot, diced

2 cloves garlic, minced

1 chilli pepper, finely diced

15 g (½ oz) tomato paste

600 g (1.25 lb) can chopped tomatoes

1 tsp sugar

2 green onions, thinly sliced

15 g (½ oz) coriander (cilantro), chopped

2 tbsp olive oil

salt & pepper to taste

METHOD

- Preheat the oven to 200°C (400°F).
- Place the tofu into a bowl and toss with 1 tablespoon of olive oil, and season with salt and pepper. Spread on a baking sheet and bake for 20 minutes until crispy.
- Heat another 1 tablespoon of olive oil in a skillet, add the shallot, garlic and chilli pepper, and sauté for 1–2 minutes until fragrant.
- Stir in the tomato paste, cook for 1 minute, then add the canned tomatoes, 60 ml (2 fl oz) water, and sugar.
- Simmer for 10 minutes until the tomatoes break down.
- Fold in most of the green onions and coriander (cilantro), reserving some for garnish.
- Adjust seasoning, then serve topped with crispy tofu and remaining green onions and coriander (cilantro).

Tip: Serve with steamed broccolini to get in your 5 a day serves of veggies.

ENERGY	CARBS	PROTEIN	FAT
354 kcal (354 Cal)	20 g (0.7 oz)	19 g (0.7 oz)	22 g (0.8 oz)

SERVES 4 | 29 MINUTES

Pumpkin & Red Lentil Soup

INGREDIENTS

1 yellow onion, finely sliced

1 kg (2 lb) pumpkin, peeled & cubed

150 g (5 oz) red lentils, washed & drained

1L (2 pt) vegetable stock

1 tbsp fresh ginger, finely grated

1 tbsp olive oil

1 tsp sea salt

METHOD

- Heat 1 tablespoon of olive oil in a soup pot, over medium heat. Add the onion.
- Sauté for 3–5 minutes until softened.
- Add the pumpkin, lentils, stock and ginger.
- Stir, then bring to a simmer.
- Cook for around 15 minutes until the pumpkin and lentils are soft.
- Season with 1 teaspoon of sea salt. Blend until smooth and serve warm.

Tip: Batch cook and have on hand for a quick dinner or lunch anytime.

ENERGY	CARBS	PROTEIN	FAT
264 kcal (264 Cal)	45 g (1.6 oz)	12 g (0.4 oz)	4 g (0.1 oz)

SERVES 12 | 1 HOUR 35 MINUTES

Caramel Coconut Cheesecake

INGREDIENTS

100 g (3½ oz) pitted dates, soaked in hot water for 10 minutes & drained

100 g (3½ oz) almonds

60 g (2 oz) spelt flour

30 g (1 oz) plant based butter

425 g (15 oz) plant-based cream cheese

200 ml (7 fl oz) canned coconut milk

150 g (5 oz) raw coconut sugar

30 g (1 oz) cornstarch

1 tsp vanilla extract

Salted Date Caramel (page 42), to serve, (optional)

METHOD

- Preheat the oven to 170°C (340°F). Line a 18 cm (7 inch) circular baking pan.
- In a food processor, blend the dates, almonds, flour and butter until well combined. Press the mixture into the lined baking pan.
- Bake the crust for 20 minutes.
- Meanwhile, combine the cream cheese, coconut milk, coconut sugar, cornstarch and vanilla extract.
- Pour the filling over the pre-baked crust.
- Bake for an additional 60 minutes.
- For the caramel topping, prepare the Salted Date Caramel and serve over cheesecake.

ENERGY	CARBS	PROTEIN	FAT
310 kcal (310 Cal)	31 g (1.1 oz)	6 g (0.2 oz)	18 g (0.6 oz)

SERVES 16 | 15 MINUTES

Salted Date Caramel

INGREDIENTS

16 medjool dates, pitted

1 tsp vanilla extract

175–250 ml (6–8 fl oz) unsweetened almond milk

1 tsp sea salt

METHOD

- Combine the dates, 1 teaspoon of sea salt, vanilla extract and 175 ml (6 fl oz) of almond milk in a high speed blender or food processor.
- Blend until the mixture is completely smooth.
- If needed, add more almond milk, 1–2 tablespoons at a time, to aid blending or achieve the desired caramel consistency.
- Use immediately or store in the refrigerator to use later.

ENERGY	CARBS	PROTEIN	FAT
76 kcal (76 Cal)	18 g (0.6 oz)	1 g (0.03 oz)	0 g (0 oz)

SERVES 2 | 5 MINUTES

Spiced Banana & Cinnamon Smoothie

INGREDIENTS

2 bananas

60 g (2 oz) pitted dates

500 ml (1 pt) unsweetened almond milk

2 tsp chia seeds

½ tsp ground cardamom

½ lime, juiced

4 ice cubes

pinch of ground cinnamon

pinch of salt

METHOD

- Place all ingredients into a high speed blender and blend until smooth.
- Divide the smoothie between 2 glasses and garnish with a sprinkle of cinnamon and salt.
- Serve immediately.

Tip: Add a scoop of vegan protein powder to help reach your protein goals.

ENERGY	CARBS	PROTEIN	FAT
264 kcal (264 Cal)	53 g (1.9 oz)	4 g (0.1 oz)	4 g (0.1 oz)

WEEK 2 MEAL PLAN

DAY	BREAKFAST	LUNCH	SNACK	DINNER
Monday	Creamy Seed Oatmeal Bowl	Quinoa & Lentils with Garlicky Pumpkin Seeds	Keto Almond Orange Cookies, Refreshing Green Juice	Herby Green Risotto
Tuesday	Creamy Seed Oatmeal Bowl	Silky Broccoli & Pea Soup	Keto Almond Orange Cookies, Refreshing Green Juice	Herby Green Risotto
Wednesday	Tofu Scramble on Avo Toast	Silky Broccoli & Pea Soup	Keto Almond Orange Cookies, Refreshing Green Juice	Vegetable Rice Bake
Thursday	Tofu Scramble on Avo Toast	Broccoli Steak with Beetroot Hummus	Almond Orange Cookies, Refreshing Green Juice	Vegetable Rice Bake
Friday	Smashed Edamame Toast	Broccoli Steak with Beetroot Hummus	Keto Almond Orange Cookies, Refreshing Green Juice	Quinoa Tomato Coconut Curry
Saturday	Smashed Edamame Toast	Rustic White Bean Stew	Keto Almond Orange Cookies, Refreshing Green Juice	Meal Out – Enjoy!
Sunday	Refreshing Green Juice	Quinoa & Lentils with Garlicky Pumpkin Seeds	Keto Almond Orange Cookies, Refreshing Green Juice	Creamy Coconut Udon with Mushroom

SHOPPING LIST – WEEK 2

PRODUCE

2 apples of choice
4 green apples
1 avocado
2 figs
3 limes
2 lemons
Pack of blackberries
5 onions
3 shallots
3 bulbs garlic
Ginger
1 red chilli
8 celery stalks
1 cucumber
2 carrots
3 cooked beets
3 zucchini (courgettes)
Pack of green beans
2 heads broccoli
20 tenderstem broccoli spears
500 g (1 lb) mushrooms
Pack of baby spinach
Basil
Coriander (cilantro)
Mint
Parsley

PROTEIN

750 g (1½ lb) firm tofu
425 g (15 oz) extra-firm tofu
Edamame beans
Green peas (garden peas)
Vegan parmesan cheese
Vegan cheese
Almonds
Chickpeas (425 g/15 oz can)
White beans (2 x 425 g/15 oz cans)

DRY GOODS

Rolled oats
Basmati rice
Risotto rice
Coconut water
Almond flour (ground almonds)
Coconut flakes
Pecans
Chia seeds
Hemp seeds
Pumpkin seeds
Quinoa
Mixed seeds (e.g. pumpkin, sunflower)
Udon noodles
Panko breadcrumbs
Nutritional yeast
Sliced multigrain bread

STAPLES & MISC

All-purpose flour (plain flour)
Baking soda (bicarbonate of soda)
Almond extract
Orange extract
Dark chocolate chips
Paprika
Red pepper flakes (chilli flakes)
Coriander seeds
Coconut oil
Sesame oil
Agave syrup
Maple syrup
Tomato paste (purée)
Red curry paste
Brown rice miso paste
Tahini
Tamari sauce
Balsamic vinegar
Almond butter
Pickled onions
Fried onions
Basil pesto (vegan)
Ice cubes
Ground cardamom
Ground cinnamon
Ground cumin
Ground turmeric
Garlic powder
Onion powder

SERVES 4 | 15 MINUTES

Creamy Seed Oatmeal Bowl

INGREDIENTS

For the porridge:

200 g (7 oz) rolled oats

100 g (3½ oz) mixed seeds (e.g. pumpkin, sunflower)

1 tsp ground cinnamon

500 ml (1 pt) almond milk, unsweetened

pinch of salt

To serve:

2 figs

1 apple, coarsely grated

200 g (7 oz) blackberries

sprinkle of pumpkin seeds (optional)

drizzle of maple syrup (optional)

METHOD

- Add the oats, seeds, cinnamon, almond milk (or water), and a pinch of salt to a saucepan.
- Cook over medium heat for 10–15 minutes, stirring frequently, until the oats soften.
- Add more milk to taste if necessary.
- Divide the porridge into bowls and top with figs, grated apple, blackberries and pumpkin seeds.
- Drizzle with maple syrup. If desired, add a splash of cold milk before serving.

Tip: Add a scoop of vegan protein powder to help reach your protein goals.

ENERGY	CARBS	PROTEIN	FAT
438 kcal (438 Cal)	55 g (1.9 oz)	14 g (0.5 oz)	18 g (0.6 oz)

SERVES 4 | 25 MINUTES

Tofu Scramble on Avo Toast

INGREDIENTS

500 g (1 lb) firm tofu

¼ tsp ground turmeric

½ tsp garlic powder

½ tsp onion powder

¼ tsp paprika

1 tbsp tahini

2 tbsp nutritional yeast

125 ml (4 fl oz) oat milk

4 sliced bread, toasted (to serve)

1 avocado, mashed (to serve)

chopped parsley (to serve)

black pepper

1 tbsp olive oil

salt & pepper to taste

METHOD

- Drain the tofu for 15 minutes to remove excess water.
- Add the turmeric, garlic powder, onion powder, paprika, black pepper, tahini and nutritional yeast to a bowl and gradually whisk in the oat milk to form a smooth sauce.
- Crumble the pressed tofu into medium chunks using your hands.
- Heat 1 tbsp olive oil in a large non-stick skillet, over medium- high heat.
- Add the tofu and sauté for 5–7 minutes, stirring occasionally, until lightly browned.
- Pour the sauce over the tofu and stir to coat evenly.
- Cook for another 1–2 minutes or until the desired texture is achieved.
- Season with salt and pepper, and serve warm over toasted bread and smashed avocado, topped with parsley.

ENERGY	CARBS	PROTEIN	FAT
358 kcal (358 Cal)	22 g (0.8 oz)	18 g (0.6 oz)	22 g (0.8 oz)

SERVES 6 | 10 MINUTES

Homemade Pickled Red Onions

INGREDIENTS

2 large red onions, thinly sliced

1 tsp whole peppercorns

1 garlic clove, peeled

250 ml (8 fl oz) white vinegar

250 ml (8 fl oz) water

2 tbsp cane sugar

1 tbsp salt

METHOD

- Thinly slice the onions and place them in a mason jar along with the peppercorns and garlic.
- In a small pot, combine the white vinegar, water, sugar, and salt.
- Heat over medium heat, stirring until the sugar and salt dissolve (about 3 minutes).
- Let the liquid cool slightly, then pour it over the onions in the jar. Ensure the onions are fully submerged.
- Allow the jar to cool to room temperature before sealing.
- Store in the refrigerator.
- Thinly sliced onions will be ready to eat within 1 hour. For thicker slices, let them sit in the fridge overnight. The pickled onions can be stored in the refrigerator for up to 2 weeks.
- **Suggested Pairing:** These pickled onions pair perfectly with recipes like Smashed Edamame Toast (page 55) or Quinoa & Lentils with Garlicky Pumpkin Seeds (page 63).

ENERGY	CARBS	PROTEIN	FAT
52 kcal (52 Cal)	12 g (0.4 oz)	1 g (0.03 oz)	0 g (0 oz)

SERVES 4 | 10 MINUTES

Smashed Edamame Toast

INGREDIENTS

4 tbsp tahini

375 g (12 oz) frozen edamame, defrosted

½ medium ripe avocado

1½ tbsp tamari sauce

2 cloves garlic, roughly chopped

1 handful coriander (cilantro) leaves

1 tsp sesame oil

1 lime, zested & juiced

salt

For serving:

4 slices multigrain bread, toasted

4 tbsp hemp seeds

4 portions Homemade Pickled Red Onions (page 52)

METHOD

- Place the tahini, edamame, avocado, tamari, garlic, coriander (cilantro), sesame oil, lime juice and zest into a food processor. Blend to form a chunky dip consistency. Season to taste with salt.
- Toast bread slices, spread the edamame mixture over each slice.
- To serve, sprinkle with hemp seeds and top with pickled Onions.

Storage: Store the spread in an airtight container in the refrigerator for 7–10 days. The colour may fade but the flavour will remain.

ENERGY	CARBS	PROTEIN	FAT
465 kcal (465 Cal)	40 g (1.4 oz)	20 g (0.7 oz)	25 g (0.9 oz)

SERVES 2 | 25 MINUTES

Silky Broccoli & Pea Soup

INGREDIENTS

½ onion, peeled & diced

1 clove garlic, minced

1 broccoli, cut into florets & stems separated

375 ml (12 fl oz) vegetable stock

300 ml (10 fl oz) coconut water

200 g (7 oz) frozen green peas

45 g (1½ oz) almond flour

30 g (1 oz) chia seeds, plus extra for garnish

1 tbsp olive oil

salt & pepper to taste

METHOD

- Heat 1 tbsp olive oil in a large pot over medium heat. Add the diced onion and garlic.
- Cook for 5 minutes until translucent.
- Add the broccoli stems, vegetable stock and coconut water to the pot.
- Simmer for 8–10 minutes.
- Stir in the broccoli florets, green peas, almond flour and chia seeds.
- Cook for an additional 5 minutes.
- Blend the soup until smooth using an immersion blender.
- Season with salt and pepper to taste.
- Serve hot, garnished with chia seeds.

ENERGY	CARBS	PROTEIN	FAT
515 kcal (515 Cal)	56 g (2.0 oz)	21 g (0.7 oz)	23 g (0.8 oz)

SERVES 6 | 45 MINUTES

Herby Green Risotto

INGREDIENTS

2 onions, peeled & diced

3 cloves garlic, minced

4 celery stalks, chopped

425 g (15 oz) risotto rice

1 broccoli, florets finely sliced

1L (2 pt) vegetable stock

2 medium zucchini (courgettes), grated

200 g (7 oz) frozen green peas

100 g (3½ oz) basil pesto (vegan)

splash of almond milk

1 tbsp olive oil

pinch of sea salt

METHOD

- Heat 1 tbsp olive oil in a large pan over medium heat. Add onions, garlic, celery and a pinch of sea salt and cook for 5–10 minutes, stirring occasionally, until softened.
- Add the risotto rice and broccoli to the pan. Stir and cook for 2 minutes.
- Add a quarter of the hot stock to the rice, stirring constantly.
- Simmer for 20–25 minutes, gradually adding more stock as the rice absorbs the liquid.
- When the rice is tender, stir in the zucchini (courgettes), peas and basil pesto. Mix well and heat through. Add almond milk if the mixture becomes too thick.
- Divide between bowls and top with optional garnishes (not included in nutritional breakdown).

Serving suggestion: basil, parsley, flaked almonds.

Tip: Add some Creamy Tofu Ricotta (page 76) for additional flavour and protein boost.

ENERGY	CARBS	PROTEIN	FAT
433 kcal (433 Cal)	75 g (2.6 oz)	13 g (0.5 oz)	9 g (0.3 oz)

SERVES 4 | 40 MINUTES

Broccoli Steak with Beetroot Hummus

INGREDIENTS

For the beetroot hummus:

250 g (9 oz) cooked beets

425 g (15 oz) canned chickpeas (retain some liquid)

4 tbsp tahini

1 tbsp ground cumin

juice of 1 lemon

2 cloves garlic

For the broccoli steaks:

1 large broccoli, cut into 4 steaks

salt & pepper

1 tbsp olive oil

For the vinaigrette:

3 tbsp olive oil

2 tbsp balsamic vinegar

1 tsp red chilli, finely chopped

2 tbsp fresh parsley, chopped

1 tsp agave syrup

salt & pepper to taste

METHOD

- Prepare the beetroot hummus by blending the beets, chickpeas, tahini, cumin, lemon juice, garlic and a splash of chickpea liquid in a food processor until smooth. Season with salt.
- Heat 1 tbsp olive oil in a frying pan over medium-high heat.
- Sear the broccoli steaks on each side for 5 minutes, until tender and golden. Season with salt and pepper.
- For the vinaigrette, whisk together olive oil, balsamic vinegar, chilli, parsley and agave syrup.
- Season to taste with salt & pepper.
- To serve, spread the hummus on a plate, top with broccoli steaks and drizzle over vinaigrette.

ENERGY	CARBS	PROTEIN	FAT
342 kcal (342 Cal)	40 g (1.4 oz)	14 g (0.5 oz)	14 g (0.5 oz)

SERVES 4 | 20 MINUTES

Quinoa & Lentils with Garlicky Pumpkin Seeds

INGREDIENTS

For the quinoa:

175 g (6 oz) uncooked quinoa

300 ml (10 fl oz) water

pinch of salt

For the garlicky pumpkin seeds:

4 garlic cloves, thinly sliced

2 tsp coriander seeds, lightly crushed

75 g (2½ oz) pumpkin seeds

½–1 tsp red pepper flakes, to taste

2 tbsp olive oil

salt & pepper to taste

To assemble:

175 g (6 oz) pre-cooked lentils

2 portions of Creamy Tofu Ricotta (page 76)

4 portions of Homemade Pickled Red Onions (page 52)

METHOD

- Bring 300 ml (10 fl oz) water to a boil in a medium pot.
- Add a pinch of salt and the quinoa. Reduce heat to low, cover, and cook for 12 minutes or until the water is absorbed. Fluff with a fork and set aside.
- Heat 2 tbsp olive oil in a pot over medium heat, add the garlic and cook for 1 minute.
- Stir in coriander and pumpkin seeds and cook for another 2–3 minutes.
- Add red pepper flakes and season with salt in the last 30 seconds. Remove from heat.
- To assemble, layer the quinoa, lentils and ricotta in a bowl.
- Top with the garlicky pumpkin seeds and pickled onions.
- Serve warm or at room temperature.

ENERGY	CARBS	PROTEIN	FAT
515 kcal (515 Cal)	54 g (1.9 oz)	23 g (0.8 oz)	23 g (0.8 oz)

SERVES 3 | 30 MINUTES

Creamy Coconut Udon with Mushrooms

INGREDIENTS

300 g (10 oz) block of firm tofu, drained & cut into bite-sized pieces

3 shallots, finely sliced

2 garlic cloves, crushed or grated

2 cm (¾ inch) piece ginger, peeled & grated

200 g (7 oz) mushrooms

3 tbsp brown rice miso paste

425 ml (15 fl oz) coconut milk, lite

500 ml (1 pt) hot vegetable stock

100 g (3½ oz) dry udon noodles

150 g (5 oz) baby spinach, roughly chopped

1–2 limes, zested & juiced

METHOD

- Heat 1 tbsp olive oil in a large skillet over medium-high heat.
- Add the tofu and cook for 10–12 minutes, turning occasionally, until golden and crispy. Set aside on kitchen paper.
- In a large wok, heat another 1 tbsp olive oil over medium- high heat. Add the shallots, garlic, ginger and mushrooms, cook for 8–10 minutes until soft and fragrant.
- Stir in the miso paste, coconut milk and vegetable stock.
- Bring to a boil.
- Add the udon noodles, cover and cook for 8–10 minutes, or until the noodles are tender.
- Add the spinach and cooked tofu to the saucepan. Stir through and divide the mixture between bowls.
- Garnish with lime juice, zest, and season to taste with salt and pepper. Serve warm.

ENERGY	CARBS	PROTEIN	FAT
481 kcal (481 Cal)	43 g (1.5 oz)	21 g (0.7 oz)	25 g (0.9 oz)

SERVES 3 | 30 MINUTES

Quinoa Tomato Coconut Curry

INGREDIENTS

1 tbsp coconut oil

½ onion, diced

2 garlic cloves, minced

15 g (½ oz) fresh ginger, grated

60 g (2 oz) red curry paste

200 g (7 oz) quinoa

100 g (3½ oz) tomato paste

200 ml (7 fl oz) coconut milk, lite

500 ml (1 pt) vegetable stock

½ zucchini (courgettes), diced

150 g (5 oz) green beans, trimmed

100 g (3½ oz) frozen green peas

15 g (½ oz) fresh coriander (cilantro), chopped

METHOD

- Heat the coconut oil in a large pot over medium heat. Sauté the onion, garlic and ginger for 3 minutes.
- Add the curry paste.
- Cook for 2 minutes.
- Stir in the quinoa, tomato paste, coconut milk and vegetable stock.
- Bring to a boil, then reduce heat to a simmer for 15 minutes.
- Add the zucchini (courgettes), green beans and peas.
- Continue cooking for 10 minutes, or until the vegetables are tender.
- Serve in bowls, garnished with coriander (cilantro) and a drizzle of coconut milk.

ENERGY	CARBS	PROTEIN	FAT
458 kcal (458 Cal)	67 g (2.4 oz)	16 g (0.6 oz)	14 g (0.5 oz)

SERVES 4 | 30 MINUTES

Rustic White Bean Stew

INGREDIENTS

1 large onion, thinly sliced

1 tbsp garlic, minced

375 ml (12 fl oz) vegetable stock

2x 425 g (15 oz) cans white beans (e.g. cannellini), drained

30 g (1 oz) basil leaves

250 g (8 oz) baby spinach leaves

115 g (4 oz) vegan

Parmesan cheese, shredded

2 tbsp olive oil

salt & pepper to taste

METHOD

- Heat 2 tbsp olive oil in a large pot over medium-low heat.
- Add the onions and garlic, cook for 10–15 minutes, stirring occasionally, until soft and golden.
- Stir in the vegetable stock, scraping any browned bits from the bottom of the pot.
- Add the beans, bring to a boil, then reduce to a simmer for 5 minutes.
- Add basil and spinach, stirring until wilted. Season with salt and pepper.
- Stir in Parmesan and drizzle with olive oil before serving.
- Alternatively, garnish individual portions with Parmesan and olive oil.

ENERGY	CARBS	PROTEIN	FAT
320 kcal (320 Cal)	27 g (1.0 oz)	17 g (0.6 oz)	16 g (0.6 oz)

SERVES 2 | 45 MINUTES

Vegetable Rice Bake

INGREDIENTS

60 g (6 oz) basmati rice

300 g (10 oz) frozen broccoli

250 g (8 oz) mushrooms, quartered

1 onion, thinly sliced

2 carrots, sliced

2 tbsp all purpose flour

160 ml (5 fl oz) vegetable stock

100 ml (3 fl oz) oat milk

60 g (2 oz) shredded vegan cheese, divided

15 g (½ oz) panko breadcrumbs

15 g (½ oz) fried onions

METHOD

- Preheat the oven to 180°C (320°F). Cook the rice according to the package instructions.
- Boil the broccoli in salted water for 3–5 minutes until tender but still firm. Drain and set aside.
- Heat 1 tbsp olive oil in a pan over medium heat, add the mushrooms, onions and a pinch of salt.
- Sauté for 5 minutes.
- Add the carrots and cook for 4–5 minutes. Stir in flour and cook for 1 minute.
- Now add the vegetable stock, broccoli and rice to the pan.
- Mix well, then transfer to a casserole dish. Pour in oat milk and half the vegan cheese. Season with salt and pepper.
- Combine the panko breadcrumbs with the fried onions and remaining cheese. Sprinkle the mixture over the casserole.
- Bake in the oven for 25 minutes until crispy and golden.
- Serve warm.

ENERGY	CARBS	PROTEIN	FAT
492 kcal (492 Cal)	73 g (2.6 oz)	14 g (0.5 oz)	16 g (0.6 oz)

SERVES 12 | 22 MINUTES

Low-Carb Almond Orange Cookies

INGREDIENTS

250 g (8 oz) almond flour

½ tsp baking soda

60 ml (2 fl oz) coconut oil, melted & slightly cooled

100 g (3½ oz) maple syrup

½ tsp almond extract

½ tsp orange extract

100 g (3½ oz) dark chocolate

pinch of salt

METHOD

- Preheat the oven to 175°C (350°F). Line a baking sheet with baking paper.
- In a bowl, mix the almond flour, baking soda, coconut oil, maple syrup, almond extract, orange extract and a pinch of salt until a dough forms.
- Portion the dough into balls (about 2 tbsp each) and place on the baking sheet, spacing them 8 cm (3 inches) apart.
- Press down to flatten slightly.
- Bake the cookies for 11–12 minutes, or until golden. Remove from the oven and set on a wire rack to cool for 10 minutes.
- Melt the chocolate in a double boiler, or microwave in 30 second intervals.
- Drizzle the chocolate over the cookies and refrigerate for 15 minutes until set.

ENERGY	CARBS	PROTEIN	FAT
208 kcal (208 Cal)	4 g (0.1 oz)	12 g (0.4 oz)	16 g (0.6 oz)

SERVES 4 | 10 MINUTES

Green Juice Quencher

INGREDIENTS

1 cucumber, chopped

4 celery stalks, sliced

4 green apples, cut into wedges

30 g (1 oz) fresh mint leaves

30 g (1 oz) ginger, peeled & diced

ice cubes

METHOD

- Place the cucumber, celery, apples, mint and ginger into a high speed blender, and blend until smooth.
- Strain through a fine mesh sieve, then serve over ice, with a garnish of mint leaves or cucumber slices.

ENERGY	CARBS	PROTEIN	FAT
133 kcal (133 Cal)	29 g (1.0 oz)	2 g (0.07 oz)	1 g (0.03 oz)

SERVES 4 | 10 MINUTES

Creamy Tofu Ricotta

INGREDIENTS

425 g (15 oz) block of extra-firm tofu, drained

30 g (1 oz) nutritional yeast

½ tsp garlic powder

½ tsp onion powder

1½ tbsp extra virgin olive oil

zest of 1 medium lemon

1 tbsp lemon juice, plus more to taste

1 heaped tsp salt

black pepper

METHOD

- Drain the tofu and press gently to remove excess water.
- Crumble the tofu into the bowl of a food processor.
- Add the remaining ingredients with an additional 1 heaped tsp salt, some black pepper, and the extra virgin olive oil, then blend the mixture until it becomes creamy and smooth, pausing to scrape down the sides of the bowl as needed.
- Taste the ricotta and adjust the seasoning to taste by adding more lemon juice or salt.

ENERGY	CARBS	PROTEIN	FAT
154 kcal (154 Cal)	3 g (0.1 oz)	13 g (0.5 oz)	10 g (0.4 oz)

WEEK 3 MEAL PLAN

DAY	BREAKFAST	LUNCH	SNACK	DINNER
Monday	Almond Quinoa Granola	Velvety Zucchini Soup	3-Ingredient Pecan Cookies	Creamy Broccoli Pasta
Tuesday	Tempeh Bacon & Veggie Breakfast Bowl	Velvety Zucchini Soup	3-Ingredient Pecan Cookies	20-Minute Udon Stir-Fry
Wednesday	Tempeh Bacon & Veggie Breakfast Bowl	20-Minute Udon Stir-Fry	Tropical Mango Chia Bowl	Spicy Tom Kha Soup
Thursday	Tropical Mango Chia Bowl	Zesty Clementine Rice Salad	Almond & Banana Power Smoothie	Spicy Tom Kha Soup
Friday	Savoury Pancakes with Avocado Spread	Zesty Clementine Rice Salad	Almond & Banana Power Smoothie	Miso Potato & Cabbage Salad
Saturday	Savoury Pancakes with Avocado Spread	Miso Potato & Cabbage Salad	3-Ingredient Pecan Cookies	Meal Out – Enjoy!
Sunday	Almond Quinoa Granola	Balsamic Glazed Mushroom & Zucchini	3-Ingredient Pecan Cookies	Creamy Broccoli Pasta

WEEKLY SHOPPING LIST

PRODUCE

3 avocados

3 limes

8 clementines

3 large onions

1 leek

250 g (8 oz) red cabbage

Bunch of green onions (spring onions)

3 shallots

Ginger

Red chilli

1 lemongrass stalk

2 kg (4 lb) zucchini (courgettes)

750 g (1½ lb) baby potatoes

100 g (3½ oz) white mushrooms

425 g (15 oz) shiitake mushrooms

1 cucumber

1 broccoli

200 g (7 oz) frozen peas

100 g (3½ oz) frozen spinach

1 mango

1 banana

Rocket (arugula)

Garlic

Thyme

Mixed salad greens

Kale

Spinach

Basil

Dates

Almond butter

Coriander (cilantro)

Pomegranate seeds

200 g (7 oz) udon noodles, cooked

175 g (6 oz) pecans

200 g (7 oz) raw almonds

Pistachios

PROTEIN

250 g (8 oz) tempeh

375 g (12 oz) firm tofu

Natural soy yogurt

DRY GOODS

Rolled oats

Quinoa

Wheat flour

1 can chickpeas

Coconut sugar

Unflavoured or vanilla plant protein powder

Penne pasta (250g/8 oz)

Chia seeds

Sesame seeds

Baking powder

Dried mint

Cayenne pepper

Chilli powder

Onion powder

Smoked paprika

Curry powder

Ground cinnamon

STAPLES & MISC

Toasted sesame oil

Tamari

Ketjap manis

Thai red curry paste

Vegetable stock

(2 L /4 pt)

Coconut milk (400 ml /13 fl oz reduced fat)

Maple syrup

Coconut oil

Vegetable stock cube

¼ tsp vanilla extract

Liquid smoke

Rice (precooked or fresh)

SERVES 4 | 25 MINUTES

Smoky Maple-Glazed Tempeh Bacon

INGREDIENTS

230 g (8 oz) tempeh, thinly sliced (about 0.3 cm / ¼ inch thick)

For the marinade:

2½ tsp toasted sesame oil

1½ tbsp maple syrup

3 tbsp tamari

2½ tsp liquid smoke

½ tsp onion powder

¾ tsp smoked paprika

2½ tbsp olive oil

1½ tbsp rice vinegar

¼ tsp salt

METHOD

- For the marinade, whisk 1 tbsp olive oil, sesame oil, 1½ tbsp rice vinegar, maple syrup, tamari, liquid smoke, ¼ tsp salt, onion powder, and paprika in a medium bowl.
- Place sliced tempeh in a Ziploc bag or shallow dish, pour marinade over, and coat evenly. Refrigerate for 1–8 hours, flipping occasionally.
- Heat 1 tbsp olive oil in a nonstick pan over medium heat. Fry half the marinated tempeh in a single layer. Cook 3–4 minutes per side or until crisp, brushing with marinade before flipping.
- Repeat with the remaining tempeh using ½ tbsp olive oil.

Tip: For extra crispness, avoid overcrowding the pan.

ENERGY	CARBS	PROTEIN	FAT
258 kcal (258 Cal)	11 g (0.4 oz)	13 g (0.5 oz)	18 g (0.6 oz)

SERVES 10 | 35 MINUTES

Almond Quinoa Granola

INGREDIENTS

140 g (5 oz) rolled oats

100 g (3½ oz) uncooked quinoa

200 g (7 oz) raw almonds, roughly chopped

1 tbsp coconut sugar

3½ tbsp coconut oil

60 ml (2 fl oz) maple syrup

pinch of salt

METHOD

- Preheat the oven to 170°C (340°F).
- Combine oats, quinoa, almonds, coconut sugar and a pinch of salt in a large bowl.
- Warm coconut oil and maple syrup in a small saucepan over medium heat for 2–3 minutes, whisking until combined.
- Pour over dry ingredients and mix well.
- Spread mixture evenly on a baking sheet.
- Bake for 20 minutes, stir, then bake for 5–10 minutes more, rotating the pan to ensure even baking. Watch closely to avoid burning.
- Cool completely before serving.
- Store in a sealed container for up to 2 weeks at room temperature or 1 month in the freezer.

ENERGY	CARBS	PROTEIN	FAT
272 kcal (272 Cal)	25 g (0.9 oz)	7 g (0.2 oz)	16 g (0.6 oz)

SERVES 2 | 30 MINUTES

Savoury Pancakes with Avocado Salsa

INGREDIENTS

100 g (3½ oz) wheat flour

¼ tsp baking powder

175 ml (6 fl oz) soy milk

1 avocado, halved, pitted & mashed

¼ lime, juiced

2 tbsp soy yogurt

¼ tsp chilli flakes

2 tsp sesame seeds, roasted

60 g (2 oz) mixed salad greens

pinch of salt

1 tbsp olive oil

METHOD

- Combine flour, baking powder, and a pinch of salt in a bowl.
- Gradually whisk in soy milk and 1 tbsp olive oil until smooth; small lumps are fine.
- Heat a nonstick pan over medium heat. Drop batter to make palm-sized pancakes. Flip when bubbles form on the surface and cook for 1–2 minutes. Keep warm by covering with aluminum (tin) foil.
- Mix mashed avocado with lime juice, soy yogurt, chilli flakes, and roasted sesame seeds.
- Serve pancakes topped with avocado salsa and mixed salad greens.

ENERGY	CARBS	PROTEIN	FAT
432 kcal (432 Cal)	47 g (1.7 oz)	7 g (0.2 oz)	24 g (0.8 oz)

SERVES 1 | 30 MINUTES

Tempeh Bacon & Veggie Breakfast Bowl

INGREDIENTS

1 serving of prepared Smoky Maple-Glazed Tempeh Bacon (page 81)

100 g (3½ oz) white mushrooms, sliced

30 g (1 oz) kale, chopped

¼ avocado, sliced

100 g (3½ oz) baked sweet potato

½ tsp olive oil

salt & pepper to taste

METHOD

- Heat ½ tsp olive oil in a skillet over medium heat. Sauté mushrooms for 3–4 minutes, then add kale. Cook until softened.
- Assemble the bowl with prepared Smoky Maple-Glazed Tempeh Bacon, mushrooms, kale, avocado slices, and baked sweet potato.
- Season with salt and pepper and serve immediately.

ENERGY	CARBS	PROTEIN	FAT
505 kcal (505 Cal)	41 g (1.4 oz)	20 g (0.7 oz)	29 g (1.0 oz)

SERVES 4 | 10 MINUTES

Zesty Clementine Rice Salad

INGREDIENTS

4 clementines, peeled & sliced into rounds

250 g (8 oz) cooked wholegrain rice

1 small red onion, thinly sliced

100 g (3½ oz) rocket (arugula)

15 g (½ oz) fresh mint, sliced

60 g (2 oz) roasted pistachios, chopped

60 g (2 oz) pomegranate seeds

For the dressing:

zest & juice of 2 clementines

1 tbsp red wine

3 tbsp olive oil

1 tsp maple syrup

pinch of salt

METHOD

- Whisk clementine zest and juice with red wine vinegar, maple syrup, olive oil, and a pinch of salt to make the dressing.
- Combine rice, red onion, rocket (arugula), and mint in a bowl. Toss with dressing.
- Top with clementine slices, pistachios, and pomegranate seeds. Serve immediately.

ENERGY	CARBS	PROTEIN	FAT
478 kcal (478 Cal)	70 g (2.5 oz)	9 g (0.3 oz)	18 g (0.6 oz)

SERVES 4 | 30 MINUTES

Velvety Zucchini Soup

INGREDIENTS

2 garlic cloves, minced

1 large onion, chopped

1 kg (2 lb) zucchini (courgettes), sliced into 1.5 cm (½ inch) rounds

750 ml (1½ pt) vegetable stock

250 ml (8 fl oz) water

175 ml (6 fl oz) oat cream + 1 tbsp extra for garnish

4 tsp vegan cheese, grated

1 tbsp olive oil

salt & pepper to taste

METHOD

- Heat 1 tbsp olive oil in a large pot over medium-high heat.
- Sauté garlic and onions for 3–4 minutes.
- Add zucchini, stock, and 8 fl oz water. Bring to a boil, reduce to medium heat, and simmer for 15–20 minutes.
- Blend until smooth using a stick blender. Stir in cream, season with salt, and pepper.
- Serve hot, garnished with extra cream and cheese.

ENERGY	CARBS	PROTEIN	FAT
179 kcal (179 Cal)	16 g (0.6 oz)	4 g (0.1 oz)	11 g (0.4 oz)

SERVES 4 | 25 MINUTES

Miso Potato & Cabbage Salad

INGREDIENTS

600 g (1.25 lb) baby potatoes, washed & halved

250 g (8 oz) red cabbage, cored & sliced into strips

2 green onions, sliced at an angle

4 tbsp fresh coriander (cilantro), roughly chopped

2 tsp sesame seeds

For the dressing:

1 clove garlic, peeled & grated

1 tsp (2 g) ginger, peeled & grated

1 tbsp miso paste

2 tsp rice vinegar

½ tsp coconut sugar

2 tbsp sesame oil

½ tsp chilli flakes

2 tbsp plain soy yogurt

salt

METHOD

- Boil potatoes in salted water for 10–15 minutes until tender.
- Drain and let cool.
- To make the dressing, combine garlic, ginger, miso paste, rice vinegar, sugar, sesame oil, chilli flakes, yogurt, and salt in a bowl. Mix well.
- Toss potatoes, red cabbage, and green onions with the dressing in a large bowl.
- Garnish with coriander (cilantro), sesame seeds, and additional chilli flakes, if desired.
- Serve immediately.

ENERGY	CARBS	PROTEIN	FAT
224 kcal (224 Cal)	33 g (1.2 oz)	5 g (0.2 oz)	8 g (0.3 oz)

SERVES 4 | 40 MINUTES

Balsamic Glazed Mushroom & Zucchini

INGREDIENTS

600 g (1.25 lb) zucchini (courgettes), halved lengthwise & sliced into ¼-inch half-moons

2 shallots, thinly sliced

250 g (8 oz) white button mushrooms, cleaned & sliced

250 g (8 oz) shiitake mushrooms, stems removed & sliced

1 garlic clove, minced

1 tbsp fresh thyme leaves, picked

2 tbsp olive oil

salt & pepper to taste

1 tbsp balsamic vinegar

METHOD

- Heat 1 tbsp olive oil in a large skillet over medium-high heat.
- Sauté zucchini (courgettes) and shallots for 15–20 minutes until tender and browned. Season with salt and pepper. Remove from the pan.
- Add 1 tbsp olive oil and mushrooms to the skillet.
- Cook for 8–10 minutes until browned.
- Stir in garlic, 1 tbsp balsamic vinegar, and ½ tbsp thyme.
- Cook for 1 minute.
- Return zucchini to the pan, mix well, and warm through.
- Garnish with remaining thyme and serve.

ENERGY	CARBS	PROTEIN	FAT
93 kcal (93 Cal)	16 g (0.6 oz)	5 g (0.2 oz)	1 g (0.03 oz)

SERVES 2 | 20 MINUTES

Quick & Easy Chickpea Curry

INGREDIENTS

2 cloves garlic, peeled & chopped

45 g (1½ oz) sun-dried tomatoes in oil, chopped

2 tsp curry powder

½ tsp chilli powder

250 g (8 oz) canned chickpeas, including liquid

200 ml (7 fl oz) water

4 tbsp fresh coriander (cilantro), chopped

½ lime, juiced

45 g (1½ oz) cucumber, finely diced

175 g (6 oz) natural soy yogurt

½ tsp dried mint

1 tbsp olive oil

salt & pepper to taste

METHOD

- Heat 1 tbsp olive oil in a skillet over medium heat. Sauté garlic and sun-dried tomatoes for 1 minute.
- Add curry powder and chilli powder and cook for 30 seconds.
- Add chickpeas with liquid and water.
- Simmer for 5–7 minutes.
- Stir in coriander (cilantro) and season with salt.
- Mix yogurt with lime juice, cucumber, dried mint, salt, and pepper to make raita.
- Serve chickpea curry with raita.

ENERGY	CARBS	PROTEIN	FAT
288 kcal (288 Cal)	49 g (1.7 oz)	14 g (0.5 oz)	4 g (0.1 oz)

SERVES 4 | 20 MINUTES

Creamy Broccoli Pasta

INGREDIENTS

100 g (3½ oz) broccoli, florets separated

6 green onions, trimmed & sliced

1 leek, halved lengthwise, washed & finely sliced

2 tbsp olive oil

2 cloves garlic, minced

100 g (3½ oz) frozen spinach

200 g (7 oz) frozen peas

500 g (1 lb) dried penne pasta

60 g (2 oz) vegan cheese, grated

200 ml (7 fl oz) reserved pasta cooking water

2 tbsp olive oil

salt & pepper to taste

METHOD

- Cook pasta in boiling salted water according to package instructions. Reserve 200 ml (7 fl oz) cooking water and drain pasta.
- Heat 1 tbsp of the olive oil in a pan over medium heat.
- Sauté broccoli florets, green onions, and leeks for 5 minutes.
- Add garlic, spinach, peas, salt, and pepper.
- Cook for 10 minutes, stirring often.
- Add reserved cooking water to the pan.
- Blend sauce to your preferred consistency (smooth or chunky).
- Toss pasta and broccoli tips in the sauce with the other 1 tbsp olive oil and cheese. Serve warm.

Serving suggestion: Garnish with fresh basil and some almond flakes.

ENERGY	CARBS	PROTEIN	FAT
548 kcal (548 Cal)	98 g (3.5 oz)	12 g (0.4 oz)	12 g (0.4 oz)

SERVES 2 | 30 MINUTES

Spicy Tom Kha Soup

INGREDIENTS

1 shallot, chopped
4 garlic cloves, chopped
1 thumb of grated ginger
½ red chilli, chopped
1 lemongrass stalk, bashed
1 tbsp coconut oil
2 tbsp tamari
1 tbsp rice wine vinegar
1 tbsp Thai red curry paste
1 L (2 pt) vegetable stock
400 ml (13½ fl oz) can coconut milk, reduced fat
1 tsp coconut sugar
200 g (7 oz) shiitake mushrooms, sliced
150 g (5 oz) firm tofu, cubed
1 lime, juiced
4 green onions, chopped
4 tbsp fresh coriander (cilantro), chopped
olive oil
salt & pepper to taste

METHOD

- Heat oil in a saucepan over medium heat.
- Sauté shallot, garlic, ginger, chilli and lemongrass for 3–5 minutes.
- Stir in tamari, rice wine vinegar and curry paste.
- Cook for 2–3 minutes.
- Add vegetable stock and bring to a boil.
- Simmer for 15–20 minutes, then strain the broth, then return strained broth to the pot.
- Add coconut milk, mushrooms, tofu and sugar.
- Simmer for 5–10 minutes until softened.
- Stir in lime juice, green onions, and coriander (cilantro). Season with salt and pepper.
- Serve hot, garnished with chilli oil if desired.

ENERGY	CARBS	PROTEIN	FAT
404 kcal (404 Cal)	34 g (1.2 oz)	13 g (0.5 oz)	24 g (0.8 oz)

SERVES 4 | 20 MINUTES

20-Minute Udon Stir-Fry

INGREDIENTS

200 g (7 oz) firm tofu, crumbled

200 g (7 oz) udon noodles, cooked & drained

1 small onion, grated

4 garlic cloves, grated

1 thumb of grated ginger

1 tsp chilli powder

200 ml (7 fl oz) water

1 vegetable stock cube

2 tbsp tamari

2 tbsp ketjap manis

2 tbsp rice vinegar

1 tbsp sesame oil

1 tbsp coconut sugar

125 g (4 oz) spinach

1 handful basil leaves

1 tbsp chilli oil

olive oil

salt & pepper to taste

METHOD

- Heat oil in a skillet over medium heat.
- Sauté onion, garlic, and ginger for 5 minutes until softened.
- Add chilli powder, water and stock cube.
- Cook for 2 minutes.
- Stir in crumbled tofu and cook for 5 minutes.
- Add tamari, ketjap manis, rice vinegar, sesame oil and sugar. Mix well.
- Add spinach and basil.
- Toss in cooked noodles and chilli oil.
- Season with salt and pepper.
- Serve warm.

ENERGY	CARBS	PROTEIN	FAT
319 kcal (319 Cal)	50 g (1.8 oz)	14 g (0.5 oz)	7 g (0.2 oz)

MAKES 8 | 20 MINUTES

3-Ingredient Pecan Cookies

INGREDIENTS

175 g (6 oz) pecans & 8 half pecans for garnish

150 g (5 oz) dates, pitted

2 tbsp maple syrup

METHOD

- Preheat the oven to 200°C (390°F). Line a baking sheet with parchment paper.
- Blend pecans and dates in a food processor until a coarse crumb forms.
- Transfer mixture to a bowl. Add maple syrup and mix into a dough.
- Shape into 8 balls, flatten slightly, and place on the baking sheet.
- Top each ball with a half pecan.
- Bake for 15 minutes. Let cool before serving.

ENERGY	CARBS	PROTEIN	FAT
240 kcal (240 Cal)	21 g (0.7 oz)	3 g (0.1 oz)	16 g (0.6 oz)

SERVES 2 | 15 MINUTES

Tropical Mango Chia Bowl

INGREDIENTS

2 tbsp chia seeds

125 ml (4 fl oz) coconut milk, carton

¼ tsp vanilla extract

1 mango, peeled & chopped

60 g (2 oz) coconut yogurt

1 serving of Almond Quinoa Granola

METHOD

- Combine chia seeds, milk, and vanilla extract in a container.
- Mix well and let set for at least 20 to 60 minutes, stirring every so often to prevent clumps.
- Blend the mango for a smooth puree.
- Layer the chia pudding, yogurt, mango puree, and granola in bowls.
- Serve immediately, or refrigerate until ready to eat.

Tip: Prepare the chia pudding the night before for a quick breakfast option.

ENERGY	CARBS	PROTEIN	FAT
338 kcal (338 Cal)	46 g (1.6 oz)	7 g (0.2 oz)	14 g (0.5 oz)

SERVES 1 | 5 MINUTES

Almond & Banana Power Smoothie

INGREDIENTS

1 small frozen banana

250 ml (8 fl oz) unsweetened almond milk

2 tbsp almond butter

2 tbsp unflavoured or vanilla plant-based protein powder

1 tbsp maple syrup

½ tsp ground cinnamon

METHOD

- Combine all ingredients in a blender.
- Blend until smooth and creamy.
- Serve immediately.

ENERGY	CARBS	PROTEIN	FAT
461 kcal (461 Cal)	49 g (1.7 oz)	19 g (0.7 oz)	21 g (0.7 oz)

WEEK 4 MEAL PLAN

DAY	BREAKFAST	LUNCH	SNACK	DINNER
Monday	Multi Seed Bread with Blueberry Chia Seed Jam	Chickpea Potato Soup	Chocolate Sweet Potato Smoothie	Chilli Garlic Noodles
Tuesday	Chocolate Sweet Potato Smoothie	Chilli Garlic Noodles	Crispy Carrot Cake Bites	Ground Seitan Peas Bolognese
Wednesday	Spinach Waffles with Avocado	Ground Seitan Peas Bolognese	Crispy Carrot Cake Bites	Coconut Lentil Curry
Thursday	Spinach Waffles with Avocado	Coconut Lentil Curry	Chocolate Sweet Potato Smoothie	Quinoa Stuffed Peppers
Friday	Chickpea Pancakes with Blueberry Chia Jam	Chickpea Salad with Tahini Dressing	Multi Seed Bread with Blueberry Chia Seed Jam	Quinoa Stuffed Peppers
Saturday	Chickpea Pancakes with Blueberry Chia Jam	Quinoa Bowl with Tahini Dressing	Crispy Carrot Cake Bites	Meal Out – Enjoy!
Sunday	Multi Seed Bread with Blueberry Chia Seed Jam	Chickpea Potato Soup	Chocolate Sweet Potato Smoothie	Creamy Cashew Tomato Pasta

WEEKLY SHOPPING LIST

PRODUCE

1 avocado

1 cucumber

1 tomato

3 red bell peppers

1 green bell pepper

1 yellow onion

2 red onions

1 shallot

3 green onions (spring onions)

1 carrot

1 garlic bulb

200 g (7 oz) potatoes

500 g (1 lb) sweet potatoes

500 g (1 lb) pumpkin

6 bell peppers (any colour)

Parsley

Basil

Coriander (cilantro)

2 lemons, for juice

½ chilli pepper

3 bananas

Frozen blueberries

Frozen corn

Frozen edamame

3 cans chickpeas

2 cans black beans

100 g (3½ oz) green peas

300 g (10 oz) udon noodle

600 g (1.25 lb) rigatoni pasta

PROTEIN

250 g (8 oz) ground seitan

100 g (3½ oz) vegan feta

100 g (3½ oz) vegan cheese

2 tbsp vegan Parmesan

DRY GOODS

500 g (1 lb) quinoa

200 g (7 oz) red lentils

45 g (1½ oz) psyllium husk powder

45 g (1½ oz) chia seeds

30 g (1 oz) ground flaxseed

150 g (5 oz) sunflower seeds

100 g (3½ oz) pumpkin seeds

45 g (1½ oz) hemp seeds

45 g (1½ oz) sesame seeds

100 g (3½ oz) spelt flour

100 g (3½ oz) chickpea flour

1 tbsp cornstarch (cornflour)

Packet rice cakes

STAPLES & MISC

750 ml (1½ pt) almond milk

250 ml (8 fl oz) tomato sauce (passata)

825 g (1.75 lb) diced tomatoes

60 g (2 oz) tomato paste

1.5L (3 pt) vegetable stock

200 ml (7 fl oz) coconut milk

200 g (7 oz) tahini

Tamari

Chilli garlic oil

75 g (2½ oz) pitted kalamata olives

Vanilla extract

150 g (5 oz) raw cashews

60 g (2 oz) walnuts

175 g (6 oz) medjool dates

2 tbsp raw cacao powder

60 g (2 oz) vegan white chocolate

Baking powder

Ground cinnamon

Cardamom

Ground ginger

Paprika powder

Dried rosemary

Garlic powder

Oregano

Cumin

Cumin seeds

Crushed red pepper

Turmeric

Curry powder

Cardamom pods

Star anise

Coriander seeds

MAKES 16 SLICES | 60 MINUTES

Multi-Seed Bread

INGREDIENTS

45 g (1½ oz) psyllium husk powder

45 g (1½ oz) chia seeds

30 g (1 oz) ground flaxseed

½ tsp sea salt

150 g (5 oz) raw sunflower seeds

100 g (3½ oz) raw pumpkin seeds (pepitas)

45 g (1½ oz) hemp seeds

45 g (1½ oz) sesame seeds

1 tbsp maple syrup

60 g (2 oz) tahini

300 ml (10 fl oz) water

METHOD

- Preheat the oven to 190°C (375°F). Line a standard loaf pan (21 x 12 x 6 cm / 8½ x 4½ x 2½ inches) with parchment paper.
- In a large mixing bowl, combine the psyllium husk powder, chia seeds, ground flaxseed, sea salt, sunflower seeds, pumpkin seeds, hemp seeds, sesame seeds, and maple syrup.
- Add the tahini and water, stirring until a thick dough forms.
- Transfer the dough to the prepared pan. Use your hands to spread and press it into an even layer.
- Bake for 50 minutes, or until the loaf sounds hollow when tapped. If needed, bake for a few more minutes.
- Remove from the oven and let sit for a couple of minutes. Lift the loaf out using the parchment paper and transfer it to a cooling rack.
- Cool for at least 15 minutes before slicing into 16 pieces.
- Serve with Blueberry Chia Seed Jam (page 115).

ENERGY	CARBS	PROTEIN	FAT
177 kcal (177 Cal)	9 g (0.3 oz)	6 g (0.2 oz)	13 g (0.5 oz)

SERVES 2 | 11 MINUTES

Chickpea Pancakes with Blueberry Chia Jam

INGREDIENTS

100 g (3½ oz) chickpea flour

1½ tsp baking powder

1 tbsp maple syrup

100 ml (3 fl oz) water

1 tsp vanilla extract

½ tsp cinnamon

4 tbsp Blueberry Chia Seed Jam

¼ tsp sea salt

¼ tsp olive oil

METHOD

- Preheat a non-stick frying pan over medium heat.
- In a mixing bowl, whisk together the chickpea flour, ¼ tsp sea salt, baking powder, and maple syrup.
- Add the water, vanilla extract, and cinnamon.
- Whisk until smooth. The batter will be thick. Let it rest for a few minutes while the pan heats.
- Lightly grease the pan with ¼ tsp olive oil if needed.
- Pour in 4 tbsp portions of the batter and cook for 4–5 minutes, until the edges look dry and a few bubbles form.
- Flip and cook for another 30 seconds to 1 minute, until firm and golden brown.
- Repeat with the remaining batter.
- Serve warm with Blueberry Chia Seed Jam Page 140.

ENERGY	CARBS	PROTEIN	FAT
236 kcal (236 Cal)	40 g (1.4 oz)	10 g (0.4 oz)	4 g (0.1 oz)

SERVES 2 | 15 MINUTES

Spinach Waffles with Avocado

INGREDIENTS

60 g (2 oz) baby spinach, washed

100 g (3½ oz) spelt flour

1 tbsp cornstarch (cornflour)

½ tsp baking powder

1 avocado, pitted & peeled

15 g (½ oz) bean sprouts

100 ml (3 fl oz) water

salt & pepper to taste

½ tsp cooking oil spray

METHOD

- Blend the spinach and 100 ml (3 fl oz) water until smooth.
- In a mixing bowl, whisk together the spelt flour, cornstarch, and baking powder.
- Fold in the spinach puree and mix until you have a smooth, slightly runny batter. Add more water if needed. Season with salt and pepper.
- Preheat the waffle iron.
- Lightly grease with ½ tsp cooking oil spray.
- Pour 2 tbsp of batter into the waffle iron for each waffle.
- Cook according to your waffle iron's instructions until golden brown. Carefully remove the waffles and place them on a cooling rack. Repeat with the remaining batter.
- Mash the avocado with a fork and season with salt and pepper.
- To serve, spread avocado over a waffle, top with sprouts, and repeat to create a stack.

ENERGY	CARBS	PROTEIN	FAT
401 kcal (401 Cal)	50 g (1.8 oz)	12 g (0.4 oz)	17 g (0.6 oz)

SERVES 4 | 10 MINUTES

Chocolate Sweet Potato Smoothie

INGREDIENTS

425 g (15 oz) sweet potatoes, leftover baked & peeled

750 ml (1½ pt) almond milk, unsweetened

3 bananas, frozen

2 tbsp raw cacao powder

2 tbsp maple syrup

1 tsp ground cinnamon

½ tsp ground ginger

METHOD

- In a blender, combine all ingredients and blend until smooth and creamy.
- Pour into glasses and drink straight away.

ENERGY	CARBS	PROTEIN	FAT
243 kcal (243 Cal)	50 g (1.8 oz)	4 g (0.1 oz)	3 g (0.1 oz)

SERVES 2 | 30 MINUTES

Chickpea Potato Soup

INGREDIENTS

200 g (7 oz) potatoes, peeled & finely diced

3 tbsp olive oil

250 g (8 oz) canned chickpeas, rinsed & drained

1 clove garlic, peeled & grated

600 ml (1.25 pt) vegetable stock

1 tsp paprika powder

1 tsp dried rosemary

1 tsp chilli flakes, for garnish

salt & pepper to taste

METHOD

- Blend half of the chickpeas until smooth for a creamier texture. Alternatively, mash them with a potato masher.
- Heat 2 tbsp of the olive oil in a pot over medium-high heat. Add the grated garlic and sauté for 1 minute.
- Add the diced potatoes and the remaining whole chickpeas.
- Sauté for 2–3 minutes, seasoning with salt and pepper.
- Pour in the vegetable stock and stir in the pureed chickpeas.
- Mix well.
- Add the paprika, dried rosemary, salt, and pepper. Simmer for 20 minutes until the potatoes are tender.
- Drizzle with remaining 1 tsp olive oil and garnish with chilli flakes.
- Serve immediately and enjoy!

ENERGY	CARBS	PROTEIN	FAT
460 kcal (460 Cal)	56 g (2.0 oz)	14 g (0.5 oz)	20 g (0.7 oz)

SERVES 6 | 25 MINUTES

Chickpea Salad with Tahini Dressing

INGREDIENTS

500 g (1 lb) chickpeas, drained & rinsed

1 cucumber, chopped

1 red bell pepper, chopped

½ red onion, thinly sliced

75 g (2½ oz) pitted kalamata olives, halved

75 g (2½ oz) vegan feta, crumbled

6 servings of Tahini Dressing

salt & pepper to taste

METHOD

- In a large bowl, combine the chickpeas, cucumber, bell pepper, onion, olives and feta. Season with salt and black pepper.
- Pour the Easy Tahini Dressing (page 136) over the salad and toss to coat just before serving.

ENERGY	CARBS	PROTEIN	FAT
307 kcal (307 Cal)	32 g (1.1 oz)	11 g (0.4 oz)	15 g (0.5 oz)

SERVES 4 | 1 HOUR

Quinoa Bowl with Tahini Dressing

INGREDIENTS

For the Quinoa:

255 g (9 oz) uncooked quinoa, rinsed

For the Vegetables:

1 red onion, chopped

1 green bell pepper, chopped

400 g (14 oz) pumpkin, chopped into cubes

½ tsp garlic powder

½ tsp dried oregano

1½ tsp salt

½ tsp black pepper

590ml (20 fl oz) water

3 tbsp olive oil

For Serving:

4 tbsp chopped fresh parsley

4 servings of tahini

tahini dressing

METHOD

- In a small saucepan, combine the quinoa, ½ tsp salt, and 590 ml (20 fl oz) water, and cook according to package instructions. Fluff with a fork.
- Preheat the oven to 220°C (425°F).
- Arrange the onion, bell pepper, and pumpkin on a baking tray.
- Drizzle with 3 tbsp olive oil and season with 1 tsp salt, ½ tsp black pepper, garlic powder, and oregano. Toss to coat and spread into an even layer.
- Roast for 30 minutes until fork-tender.
- Flip the vegetables and broil on high for 5 minutes for extra caramelization.
- Divide the quinoa among four bowls.
- Top with the roasted vegetables and sprinkle with fresh parsley.
- Drizzle with Easy Tahini Dressing (page 136) and serve immediately.

ENERGY	CARBS	PROTEIN	FAT
474 kcal (474 Cal)	55 g (1.9 oz)	14 g (0.5 oz)	22 g (0.8 oz)

SERVES 4 | 15 MINUTES

Chilli Garlic Noodles

INGREDIENTS

300 g (10 oz) udon noodles

1 red bell pepper, thinly sliced

3 green onions (spring onions), sliced

15 g (½ oz) fresh coriander (cilantro), chopped

175 g (6 oz) frozen edamame, defrosted

3 tbsp tamari

2 tbsp rice vinegar

½ tbsp balsamic vinegar

3 tbsp store-bought chilli garlic oil

1 tsp olive oil

½ tsp sea salt

METHOD

- In a pot, boil salted water. Cook udon according to packet instructions. Drain, rinse with cold water, and let drain.
- Heat 1 tsp olive oil in a pan and toss the bell pepper, green onions, coriander (cilantro) and edamame with ½ tsp sea salt.
- Cook for 5–6 minutes.
- In a bowl, mix tamari, rice vinegar, balsamic vinegar and chilli garlic oil.
- Pour sauce over vegetables and add udon, heat for another 2–3 minutes. Toss well.
- Enjoy at room temperature or chilled.

ENERGY	CARBS	PROTEIN	FAT
408 kcal (408 Cal)	59 g (2.1 oz)	16 g (0.6 oz)	12 g (0.4 oz)

SERVES 2 | 30 MINUTES

Ground Seitan Peas Bolognese

INGREDIENTS

150 g (5 oz) rigatoni pasta

2 tsp olive oil

1 shallot, minced

250 g (8 oz) ground seitan

1 tomato, cored & diced

1 tsp garlic, grated

½ tsp salt

250 ml (8 fl oz) tomato sauce (passata)

100 g (3½ oz) green peas

2 tbsp shredded vegan Parmesan

METHOD

- Cook rigatoni pasta in salted boiling water according to package instructions. Reserve 250 ml (8 fl oz) of the pasta water, then drain.
- Heat the olive oil in a pan over medium-high heat.
- Sauté shallot and seitan, breaking it up, until browned, about 3–4 minutes.
- Add tomato, garlic and salt. Cook for 2–3 minutes.
- Stir in tomato sauce and 125 ml (4 fl oz) of reserved pasta water. Simmer for 3–4 minutes until thickened.
- Add pasta and toss to coat. Adjust consistency with more pasta water if needed.
- Stir in peas and cook until heated through.
- Remove from heat, plate, and top with vegan Parmesan.

ENERGY	CARBS	PROTEIN	FAT
555 kcal (555 Cal)	79 g (2.8 oz)	35 g (1.2 oz)	11 g (0.4 oz)

SERVES 6 | 50 MINUTES

Quinoa Stuffed Peppers

INGREDIENTS

200 g (7 oz) uncooked quinoa, rinsed

500 ml (1 pt) vegetable stock

6 medium bell peppers, tops cut off, cores removed

1 small onion, chopped

2 garlic cloves, minced

425 g (15 oz) canned diced tomatoes

425 g (15 oz) canned black beans, drained & rinsed

150 g (5 oz) frozen corn, thawed

1 tsp cumin

1 tsp paprika

100 g (3½ oz) shredded vegan cheese

coriander (cilantro), chopped, for garnish

1 tbsp olive oil

½ tsp salt

¼ tsp black pepper

METHOD

- Simmer quinoa and stock in a pot until the liquid is absorbed, about 15 minutes. Let sit for 5 minutes, then fluff with a fork.
- Preheat the oven to 190°C (375°F). Halve the bell peppers and place them cut side up in a baking dish with a little water at the bottom.
- Heat 1 tbsp olive oil in a pan over medium heat. Sauté onion for 2–3 minutes. Add garlic and cook for 1 more minute.
- Stir in cooked quinoa, diced tomatoes, black beans, corn, cumin, paprika, ½ tsp salt, and ¼ tsp black pepper. Cook for 5 minutes.
- Fill the bell peppers with the quinoa mixture, then top with shredded cheese.
- Bake uncovered for 30–35 minutes until the peppers are tender.
- Top with chopped coriander (cilantro) and enjoy!

Storage: Refrigerate in an airtight container for 3–4 days.

ENERGY	CARBS	PROTEIN	FAT
325 kcal (325 Cal)	50 g (1.8 oz)	11 g (0.4 oz)	9 g (0.3 oz)

SERVES 2 | 30 MINUTES

Creamy Cashew Tomato Pasta

INGREDIENTS

125 g (4 oz) raw cashews

120 ml (4 fl oz) fresh water & ¼ tsp salt

500 g (1 lb) rigatoni pasta

1 yellow onion, finely chopped

4 garlic cloves, minced

56 g (2 oz) tomato paste

425 g (15 oz) canned diced tomatoes

¼ tsp red chilli flakes

handful basil, torn

2 tbsp olive oil

salt

METHOD

- Power boil cashews for 5 minutes.
- Drain, blend with the fresh water and the salt until smooth.
- Cook pasta in salted water until al dente (2–3 minutes less than package instructions). Drain, but reserve 375 ml (12 fl oz) of the pasta water.
- Heat 2 tbsp olive oil in a pan.
- Sauté onion 3–4 minutes, add garlic and cook for 1 minute.
- Stir in tomato paste, cook for 2 minutes. Add tomatoes, red chilli flakes, ½ tsp salt, and 125 ml (4 fl oz) pasta water. Simmer for 10 minutes.
- Add pasta, cashew cream, and remaining 250 ml (8 fl oz) pasta water. Toss to coat.
- Serve with basil.

ENERGY	CARBS	PROTEIN	FAT
480 kcal (480 Cal)	70 g (2.5 oz)	14 g (0.5 oz)	16 g (0.6 oz)

SERVES 4 | 30 MINUTES

Coconut Lentil Curry

INGREDIENTS

1 tbsp coconut oil

2 cardamom pods

2 star anise

2 tsp coriander seeds

1 tsp cumin seeds

1 tsp turmeric

2 tsp curry powder

1 yellow onion, finely chopped

1 garlic clove, finely chopped

2 tbsp ginger, diced

½ chilli pepper, finely diced

175 g (6 oz) red lentils

200 ml (7 fl oz) canned coconut milk

300 ml (10 fl oz) vegetable stock

150 g (5 oz) baby spinach, washed & drained

METHOD

- Heat coconut oil in a saucepan over medium heat. Add cardamom, star anise, coriander seeds, cumin seeds, turmeric and curry powder. Toast for 2–3 minutes until fragrant.
- Add onion, garlic, ginger and chilli pepper. Sauté for 5 minutes until softened.
- Stir in lentils, coconut milk, and vegetable stock. Bring to a simmer and cook for 12 minutes, stirring occasionally.
- Add spinach and cook until wilted.
- Serve hot.

ENERGY	CARBS	PROTEIN	FAT
313 kcal (313 Cal)	36 g (1.3 oz)	13 g (0.5 oz)	13 g (0.5 oz)

SERVES 8 | 5 MINUTES

Easy Tahini Dressing

INGREDIENTS

125 g (4 oz) tahini paste

80 ml (2½ fl oz) lemon juice

2 garlic cloves, pressed or grated

4 tbsp water

salt to taste

METHOD

- In a bowl, whisk together tahini, lemon juice, garlic, and ¼ tsp salt until thick.
- Gradually whisk in 4 tbsp of water until smooth and pourable.
- Adjust with more lemon juice, salt, or water to taste.

Storage: Refrigerate in an airtight container for up to 2 weeks or freeze for up to 3 months.

ENERGY	CARBS	PROTEIN	FAT
100 kcal (100 Cal)	4 g (0.1 oz)	3 g (0.1 oz)	8 g (0.3 oz)

SERVES 8 | 30 MINUTES

Carrot Cake Bites

INGREDIENTS

8 rice cakes

60 g (2 oz) walnuts

1 medium carrot, peeled & chopped

175 g (6 oz) medjool dates, pitted

1 tsp cinnamon

½ tsp ground cardamom

½ tsp ground ginger

60 g (2 oz) vegan white chocolate, melted

1 tsp melted coconut oil

METHOD

- In a food processor, pulse rice cakes, walnuts, carrot, dates, and spices until a sticky paste forms.
- If too dry, add more dates or 1 tsp melted coconut oil.
- Roll into tablespoon-sized balls and freeze for 15 minutes.
- Dip each ball in melted white chocolate.
- Let set, then enjoy or store in the fridge for up to 7 days.

Serving suggestion: Sprinkle with dark chocolate and chopped nuts or coconut flakes.

ENERGY	CARBS	PROTEIN	FAT
216 kcal (216 Cal)	33 g (1.2 oz)	3 g (0.1 oz)	8 g (0.3 oz)

SERVES 8 | 12 MINUTES

Blueberry Chia Seed Jam

INGREDIENTS

300 g (10 oz) frozen blueberries

2 tbsp chia seeds

2 tbsp maple syrup

METHOD

- Heat blueberries in a saucepan over medium heat, stirring occasionally, until thawed and juicy, about 5–7 minutes.
- Mash to desired consistency using a fork or potato masher.
- Stir in chia seeds and maple syrup. Turn off the heat and let sit for 5–10 minutes to thicken.
- Store in a sealed container in the fridge for up to 1 week.
- Enjoy with Chickpea Pancakes (page 115) and Multi-Seed Bread (page 112)

Note: 1 serving is equivalent to 2 tbsp.

ENERGY	CARBS	PROTEIN	FAT
49 kcal (49 Cal)	9 g (0.3 oz)	1 g (0.03 oz)	1 g (0.03 oz)

WEEK 5 MEAL PLAN

DAY	BREAKFAST	LUNCH	SNACK	DINNER
Monday	Sweet Potato Breakfast Burrito	Cauliflower & Coconut Soup	Banana Almond Energy Balls	Baked Tofu Fajitas
Tuesday	Sweet Potato Breakfast Burrito	Cauliflower & Coconut Soup	Banana Almond Energy Balls	Lentil & Rice Stew
Wednesday	Cinnamon Porridge with Baked Banana	Leftover Lentil & Rice Stew	Lemon Blueberry Chia Smoothie	One-Pot Mushrooms & White Beans
Thursday	Cinnamon Porridge with Baked Banana	Kale Chickpea Buddha Bowl	Roasted Garlic Hummus	One-Pot Mushrooms & White Beans
Friday	Black Forest Breakfast Bowl	Kale Chickpea Buddha Bowl	Strawberry Matcha Chia Pudding	Marinated Tofu Skewers with Roasted Garlic Hummus
Saturday	Black Forest Breakfast Bowl	Smash Chickpea Salad	Strawberry Matcha Chia Pudding	Meal Out – Enjoy!
Sunday	Scramble Tofu with Spinach & Pesto	Smash Chickpea Salad	Banana Almond Energy Balls	Baked Tofu Fajitas

WEEKLY SHOPPING LIST

PRODUCE

- 3 onions
- Avocado
- 125 g (4½ oz) kale
- 150 g (5 oz) button mushrooms
- 200 g (7 oz) spinach
- 275 g (9 oz) cauliflower
- Bulb garlic
- 3 bell peppers
- 75 g (2½ oz) cherry tomatoes
- 1–2 shallots
- Coriander (cilantro)
- 2 carrots
- 4 radishes
- 200 g (7 oz) potatoes
- 500 g (1 lb) sweet potatoes
- 100 g (3½ oz) green beans
- 2 red onions
- 1 yellow onion
- 3 lemons
- 2 limes
- 1 orange
- 100 g (3½ oz) strawberries
- 210 g (7½ oz) frozen blueberries
- 500 g (17.6 oz) frozen berry mix
- 2 bananas

PROTEIN

- 1 kg (2 lb) firm tofu
- 1 kg (2 lb) canned chickpeas
- 375 g (12 oz) canned white beans
- 300 g (10 oz) canned lentils
- 30 g (1 oz) vanilla plant-based protein powder
- Vegan sausages

DRY GOODS

- Coconut flakes
- Basmati rice
- 70 g (2½ oz) dates
- Almonds
- Almond meal
- Seed mix
- Hemp seeds
- Chia seeds
- Ground turmeric
- Curry powder
- Smoked paprika
- Ground cinnamon
- Ground coriander
- Chilli powder
- Cayenne pepper
- Garlic powder
- Onion powder
- Dried oregano
- Matcha
- Tortillas

STAPLES & MISC

- Salsa
- Unsweetened coconut yogurt
- Tamari
- Dijon mustard
- Tahini
- Almond butter
- 320 ml (11 fl oz) canned coconut milk
- 240 ml (8 fl oz) plain coconut milk (carton)
- 840 ml (28 fl oz) vegetable broth
- 500 ml (17 fl oz) almond milk, unsweetened
- Maple syrup
- Sun-dried tomato pesto

SERVES 4 | 20 MINUTES

Scrambled Tofu with Spinach & Pesto

INGREDIENTS

1 onion, diced

125 g (4 oz) spinach

500 g (1 lb) firm tofu, drained & crumbled

500 g (1 lb) can chickpeas, drained, lightly mashed with a fork

2 tsp turmeric

2 tbsp nutritional yeast

60 g (2 oz) sun-dried tomato pesto

2 tbsp olive oil

METHOD

- Heat 2 tbsp olive oil in a large skillet over medium-high heat.
- Add the onion and sauté for 4–5 minutes until softened. Add spinach and cook for 2 minutes until wilted.
- Stir in tofu, chickpeas, turmeric, and nutritional yeast. Cook, stirring, until well combined.
- Mix in sun-dried tomato pesto and cook for another 2 minutes until heated through.
- Serve immediately or with Sweet Potato Breakfast Burrito (page 146).

ENERGY	CARBS	PROTEIN	FAT
332 kcal (332 Cal)	26 g (0.9 oz)	21 g (0.7 oz)	16 g (0.6 oz)

SERVES 4 | 50 MINUTES

Sweet Potato Breakfast Burrito

INGREDIENTS

275 g (9 oz) sweet potato, cubed

1 tbsp olive oil

For the Burritos:

4 large tortillas

1 avocado, sliced

100 g (3½ oz) vegan sausages

4 tbsp salsa

4 portions of Scrambled Tofu with Spinach & Pesto (page 145)

salt & pepper to taste

METHOD

- Preheat the oven to 220°C (425°F).
- Place sweet potato on a parchment-lined baking tray. Drizzle with the olive oil, season with salt & pepper, and toss to coat. Roast for 20–25 minutes until tender.
- Meanwhile, prepare Scrambled Tofu with Spinach & Pesto (page 145) or use leftovers and fry your vegan sausages.
- Slice the sausages, then divide the roasted sweet potatoes, tofu scramble, avocado, sausages, and salsa between the tortillas.
- Fold in two sides, then roll tightly into burritos.
- Serve immediately or wrap in foil and store in the fridge for later.

ENERGY	CARBS	PROTEIN	FAT
508 kcal (508 Cal)	54 g (1.9 oz)	19 g (0.7 oz)	24 g (0.8 oz)

SERVES 2 | 13 MINUTES

Cinnamon Porridge with Baked Banana

INGREDIENTS

100 g (3½ oz) porridge oats

150 ml (5 fl oz) almond milk, unsweetened

½ tsp ground cinnamon

1 ripe banana, quartered

½ orange, zested & juiced

200 g (7 oz) natural soy yogurt

2 tsp toasted seed mix

500 ml water (1 pt)

METHOD

- In a pan, combine oats, almond milk, 500 ml (1 pt) water, and cinnamon. Bring to a boil, then reduce to low heat and cook for 5 minutes, stirring often, until thickened.
- Meanwhile, place the banana in a microwave-safe dish with orange zest and juice. Cover and microwave on high for 1½–2 minutes until softened.
- Divide the porridge between bowls and top with yogurt, baked banana, and toasted seeds.

Note: Use pre-toasted seed mix or lightly toast seeds in a dry pan for 1–2 minutes before serving.

ENERGY	CARBS	PROTEIN	FAT
355 kcal (355 Cal)	62 g (2.2 oz)	11 g (0.4 oz)	7 g (0.2 oz)

SERVES 6 | 5 MINUTES

Black Forest Breakfast Bowl

INGREDIENTS

500 g (1 lb) Black Forest frozen fruit mix, thawed

175 g (6 oz) porridge oats

750 g (1.5 lb) natural soy yogurt

3 tbsp maple syrup

6 tbsp almond butter

6 tsp seed mix

METHOD

- In a food processor, blend 300 g (10 oz) of the fruit with oats, yogurt and maple syrup until smooth using a hand blender.
- Divide the mixture between six bowls.
- Top each with the remaining fruit, almond butter, and mixed seeds.
- Serve immediately or cover and chill for up to 4 days.
- Garnish with mint leaves (optional).

ENERGY	CARBS	PROTEIN	FAT
431 kcal (431 Cal)	61 g (2.2 oz)	13 g (0.5 oz)	15 g (0.5 oz)

SERVES 2 | 30 MINUTES

Cauliflower & Coconut Soup

INGREDIENTS

300 g (10 oz) cauliflower florets

1 yellow onion, quartered

1 clove garlic, peeled

½ tsp ground cinnamon

¼ tsp chilli powder

30 g (1 oz) coconut chips

200 ml (7 fl oz) canned coconut milk

2 pt (1 L) vegetable stock

2 tbsp olive oil

salt & pepper to taste

METHOD

- Preheat the oven to 200°C (400°F).
- On a baking sheet, toss the cauliflower, onion, and garlic with 2 tbsp olive oil, cinnamon, and chilli powder. Roast for 15 minutes.
- Add coconut chips to the baking sheet and roast for 3 more minutes until golden.
- Transfer everything to a pot. Add coconut milk and vegetable stock, season with salt and black pepper, and bring to a boil.
- Reduce heat and simmer for 5 minutes.
- Blend until smooth and creamy.
- Garnish with extra coconut chips and serve.

ENERGY	CARBS	PROTEIN	FAT
335 kcal (335 Cal)	19 g (0.7 oz)	4 g (0.1 oz)	27 g (1.0 oz)

SERVES 2 | 15 MINUTES

Smash Chickpea Salad

INGREDIENTS

250 g (8 oz) chickpeas, drained

2 tbsp olive oil

½ red bell pepper, diced

75 g (2½ oz) cherry tomatoes, chopped

45 g (1½ oz) shallot, finely chopped

4 tbsp coriander (cilantro), finely chopped

30 g (1 oz) hemp seeds

½ lemon, juiced

METHOD

- Add chickpeas to a large bowl and lightly mash with a fork.
- Drizzle with the olive oil, and add the remaining ingredients. Stir to combine.
- Taste and adjust salt and pepper as needed.
- Divide into bowls and enjoy!

ENERGY	CARBS	PROTEIN	FAT
422 kcal (422 Cal)	41 g (1.4 oz)	15 g (0.5 oz)	22 g (0.8 oz)

SERVES 2 | 35 MINUTES

Lentil & Rice Stew

INGREDIENTS

1 carrot, peeled & finely chopped

200 g (7 oz) potatoes, peeled & diced

100 g (3½ oz) green beans, washed, trimmed then cut into 3 cm (1.5″) pieces

1 yellow onion, peeled & finely diced

1 tsp smoked paprika

2 pinches of cayenne pepper

½ tsp ground coriander

300 g (10 oz) canned lentils, drained

300 ml (10 fl oz) water

60 g (2 oz) basmati rice

1 tbsp olive oil

salt to season

METHOD

- Heat 1 tbsp olive oil in a pot over medium heat. Sauté carrot, potatoes, green beans, and onion for 5 minutes. Season with salt.
- Add paprika, cayenne pepper, coriander, and more salt.
- Fry for 2–3 minutes.
- Stir in lentils, rice, and water.
- Simmer for 15 minutes, adding more water if needed.
- Adjust seasoning if desired and serve.

ENERGY	CARBS	PROTEIN	FAT
468 kcal (468 Cal)	81 g (2.9 oz)	18 g (0.6 oz)	8 g (0.3 oz)

SERVES 2 | 30 MINUTES

Kale Chickpea Buddha Bowl

INGREDIENTS

200 g (7 oz) sweet potato, peeled & diced

1 red onion, sliced

60 g (2 oz) cashews, unsalted

250 g (8 oz) canned chickpeas, drained

1 tsp smoked paprika

60 g (2 oz) kale, stems removed, leaves chopped

1 carrot, sliced into ribbons

4 radishes, sliced

1 clove garlic, chopped

1 tbsp maple syrup

1 lemon, juiced

1 tbsp olive oil

salt & pepper to taste

4 tbsp water

METHOD

- Preheat the oven to 210°C (410°F).
- Toss sweet potatoes with 1 tbsp olive oil, salt, and pepper on a lined baking sheet. Roast for 20–25 minutes until tender and golden brown.
- In a small pot, cover cashews with water, bring to a boil, then reduce heat and simmer for 10–15 minutes. Drain and set aside to cool slightly.
- Toss chickpeas with smoked paprika, salt, pepper, and 1 tbsp olive oil.
- Toast in a pan over medium heat for 5 minutes until crispy.
- Place sliced onions in an ice bath for a few minutes, then drain.
- Blend cashews, garlic, maple syrup, lemon juice, salt, and 4 tbsp water until smooth.
- Gradually add more water, 1 tbsp at a time, if needed for a pourable consistency.
- In a serving bowl, massage kale with a pinch of salt.
- Add carrots, radishes, and onions, then top with roasted sweet potatoes and crispy chickpeas.
- Drizzle with cashew cream and serve.

ENERGY	CARBS	PROTEIN	FAT
348 kcal (348 Cal)	41 g (1.4 oz)	10 g (0.4 oz)	16 g (0.6 oz)

SERVES 2 | 25 MINUTES

One-Pot Mushrooms & White Beans

INGREDIENTS

150 g (5 oz) button mushrooms, sliced

375 g (12 oz) canned white beans, drained

1½ tsp curry powder

150 ml (5 fl oz) vegetable stock

125 ml (4 fl oz) canned coconut milk

125 g (4 oz) spinach

½ lemon, juiced

splash of water

salt & black pepper to taste

METHOD

- Heat a non-stick pan over medium-high heat. Add mushrooms with a splash of water and cook for 5 minutes, stirring occasionally, until browned.
- Stir in beans, curry powder, salt, and black pepper. Cook for 1 minute.
- Add vegetable stock and coconut milk. Cover and simmer on low heat for 10 minutes.
- Remove the lid, add spinach, and cook uncovered for 2–4 minutes until wilted. Adjust seasoning if needed.
- Remove from heat and stir in lemon juice. Divide into bowls and serve.

ENERGY	CARBS	PROTEIN	FAT
408 kcal (408 Cal)	55 g (1.9 oz)	20 g (0.7 oz)	12 g (0.4 oz)

SERVES 4 | 40 MINUTES

Baked Tofu Fajitas

INGREDIENTS

500 g (1 lb) firm tofu, drained, pressed & cubed

2 bell peppers (any colour), sliced

1 red onion, sliced

3 garlic cloves, minced

2 tbsp taco seasoning

lime wedges, for serving

coriander (cilantro), chopped, for serving

2 tbsp olive oil

METHOD

- Preheat the oven to 220°C (425°F).
- In a baking dish, combine tofu, bell peppers, onion, garlic, taco seasoning, and 2 tbsp olive oil.
- Toss until evenly coated and spread in a single layer.
- Bake for 25 minutes, stirring halfway through, until the tofu is golden and vegetables are tender.
- Serve with lime wedges and chopped coriander (cilantro).

ENERGY	CARBS	PROTEIN	FAT
200 kcal (200 Cal)	11 g (0.4 oz)	12 g (0.4 oz)	12 g (0.4 oz)

SERVES 4 | 1 HOUR 5 MINUTES

Marinated Tofu Skewers

INGREDIENTS

500 g (1 lb) firm tofu, drained

4 servings of Roasted Garlic Hummus (page 166)

Marinade:

2 tbsp tamari

1½ tbsp lime juice

1½ tbsp Dijon mustard

1½ tbsp maple syrup

¼ tsp cayenne pepper

¾ tsp garlic powder

¾ tsp onion powder

1 tbsp olive oil

skewers

METHOD

- If using wooden skewers, soak them in warm water for 20–30 minutes to prevent burning.
- Slice the tofu into 4 vertical slabs. Cover with a kitchen towel and weigh them down to press for 15–30 minutes. Cut into cubes.
- In a jar, combine tamari, lime juice, mustard, maple syrup, 1 tbsp olive oil, cayenne, garlic powder, and onion powder.
- Shake well to mix.
- Transfer tofu cubes to a reusable bag, pour in the marinade, and toss gently. Marinate for at least 15 minutes at room temperature or up to 8 hours in the fridge, flipping occasionally.
- Thread tofu cubes onto skewers, pressing them closely together. Reserve any excess marinade.
- Preheat the oven grill to high.
- Lightly oil a wire rack and place the skewers on top.
- Grill, rotating every 4 minutes, for a total of 16 minutes. Brush with reserved marinade as they cook.
- Remove from the oven and serve with Roasted Garlic Hummus (page 166).

ENERGY	CARBS	PROTEIN	FAT
369 kcal (369 Cal)	27 g (1.0 oz)	18 g (0.6 oz)	21 g (0.7 oz)

SERVES 4 | 30 MINUTES

Roasted Garlic Hummus

INGREDIENTS

500 g (1 lb) canned chickpeas, drained & rinsed (reserve brine)

1 garlic head

100 g (3½ oz) tahini

4 tbsp lemon juice

3 tbsp olive oil

2 ¼ tsp salt

1 ¼ tsp black pepper

tin foil

METHOD

- Preheat the oven to 200°C (400°F).
- Slice the top off the garlic head to expose the cloves. Place on a small square of foil, drizzle with 1 tbsp olive oil, ¼ tsp salt, and ¼ tsp black pepper, then wrap in foil. Roast on a baking sheet for 30–40 minutes until soft. Let cool until easy to handle.
- Add chickpeas and roasted garlic to a food processor. Start with 4 cloves and blend. Add more to taste if desired.
- Add 2 tsp salt, 1 tsp black pepper, lemon juice, 2 tbsp olive oil, and tahini. Blend while gradually adding reserved chickpea brine until smooth and creamy.
- Serve as a dip or as a side with Marinated Tofu Skewers (page 165).

ENERGY	CARBS	PROTEIN	FAT
212 kcal (212 Cal)	19 g (0.7 oz)	7 g (0.2 oz)	12 g (0.4 oz)

SERVES 12 | 10 MINUTES

Banana Almond Energy Balls

INGREDIENTS

150 g (5 oz) rolled oats

75 g (2½ oz) dates

60 g (2 oz) almonds

1 tbsp maple syrup

1 ripe banana, mashed

5 g (0.2 oz) shredded coconut

30 g (1 oz) almond meal

1 tbsp water

pinch of salt

METHOD

- In a food processor, blend mashed banana, oats, dates, almonds, maple syrup, 1 tbsp water, and a pinch of salt until combined. Add shredded coconut and pulse briefly to incorporate.
- Shape the mixture into walnut-sized balls (1 tbsp per ball).
- Roll each ball in the almond meal until evenly coated.
- Refrigerate for at least 30 minutes before serving.

ENERGY	CARBS	PROTEIN	FAT
120 kcal (120 Cal)	18 g (0.6 oz)	3 g (0.1 oz)	4 g (0.1 oz)

SERVES 2 | 1 HOUR 10 MINUTES

Strawberry Matcha Chia Pudding

INGREDIENTS

250 ml (8 fl oz) plain coconut milk (from carton)

2 tsp matcha powder

2 tbsp maple syrup, divided

½ lemon, juiced

60 g (2 oz) chia seeds

100 g (3½ oz) strawberries, chopped

250 g (8 oz) unsweetened coconut yogurt

METHOD

- In a bowl, whisk together the coconut milk, matcha powder, half of the maple syrup, and lemon juice until smooth.
- Stir in chia seeds. Let sit for 5–10 minutes, then stir again.
- Refrigerate for at least 1 hour until set.
- In a small bowl, mash strawberries with the remaining maple syrup until slightly chunky.
- Layer the mashed strawberries, coconut yogurt, and chia pudding into jars.
- Serve and enjoy or chill in the fridge for later.

Tip: Add vegan protein powder to increase protein intake.

ENERGY	CARBS	PROTEIN	FAT
294 kcal (294 Cal)	37 g (1.3 oz)	5 g (0.2 oz)	14 g (0.5 oz)

SERVES 1 | 5 MINUTES

Lemon Blueberry Chia Smoothie

INGREDIENTS

250 g (8 oz) frozen blueberries

½ frozen banana

1 tbsp chia seeds

3 tbsp fresh lemon juice

1 tsp lemon zest

1½ tsp cinnamon

375 ml (12 fl oz) almond milk, unsweetened

30 g (1 oz) vanilla plant- based protein powder

METHOD

- Add all ingredients to a high-speed blender.
- Blend on high for 30–60 seconds until completely smooth.
- Pour into a glass and enjoy.

ENERGY	CARBS	PROTEIN	FAT
416 kcal (416 Cal)	59 g (2.1 oz)	27 g (1.0 oz)	8 g (0.3 oz)

WEEK 6 MEAL PLAN

DAY	BREAKFAST	LUNCH	SNACK	DINNER
Monday	Edamame Curried Savoury Oats	Kale Quinoa Salad	Anti-Inflammatory Tropical Protein Shake	Roasted Cabbage & Crispy Chickpeas
Tuesday	Edamame Curried Savoury Oats	Kale Quinoa Salad	Chocolate Chia Flax Seed Pudding	Protein Pea Pasta
Wednesday	Chia Seed Blueberry Pancakes	Leftover Protein Pea Pasta	Chocolate Chia Flax Seed Pudding	Vegan Chickpea Chicken
Thursday	Chia Seed Blueberry Pancakes	Fresh Broccoli Salad with Mint Dressing	Anti-Inflammatory Tropical Protein Shake	Vegan Chickpea Chicken
Friday	Anti-Inflammatory Tropical Protein Shake	Fresh Broccoli Salad with Mint Dressing	Tahini Walnut Brownies	Tofu Red Curry Noodles
Saturday	Sun-Dried Tomato White Bean Dip	Fiery Carrot & Tomato Soup	Tahini Walnut Brownies	Meal Out – Enjoy!
Sunday	Vegan 'Smoked Salmon'	Fiery Carrot & Tomato Soup	Sun-Dried Tomato White Bean Dip	Tofu Red Curry Noodles

WEEKLY SHOPPING LIST

PRODUCE

4 carrots

1.13 kg (2.5 lb) tomatoes

2 yellow onions

1 red onion

1 shallot

Bunch green onions (spring onions)

3 lemons

1 lime

2 bananas

1 orange

Bunch fresh mint

Bunch fresh basil

Fresh ginger

Garlic

150 g (5 oz) kale

300 g (10 oz) cucumber

300 g (10 oz) cherry tomatoes

300 g (10 oz) broccoli

150 g (5 oz) celery

200 g (7 oz) white cabbage

75 g (2½ oz) blueberries

75 g (2½ oz) frozen edamame

500 g (1 lb) frozen peas

150 g (5 oz) frozen pineapple

150 g (5 oz) frozen mango

PROTEIN

250 g (8 oz) firm tofu

300 g (12 oz) silken tofu

1 kg (2 lb) canned chickpeas

365 g (13 oz) canned cannellini beans

Vegan cream cheese

200 g (7 oz) quinoa (uncooked)

DRY GOODS

Rolled oats

Self-raising flour

150 g (5 oz) dry ramen noodles

All-purpose flour

Instant yeast

Baking soda

Baking powder

Chia seeds

Walnuts

Nutritional yeast

Ground flaxseed

Pumpkin seeds

Croutons

Stevia powder

Sesame seeds

Unsweetened shredded coconut

Dried cranberries

Medjool dates

4 bagels

60 g (2 oz) sundried tomatoes

500 g (1 lb) pasta (of your choice)

STAPLES & MISC

Tahini

Tomato paste

Thai red curry paste

Tamari

Rice vinegar

Unsweetened almond milk

Oat milk

250 ml (8 fl oz) canned coconut milk

Vegan mayo

60 g (2 oz) sun-dried tomatoes

Sesame oil

Coconut oil

Maple syrup

Coconut sugar

Vanilla extract

Capers

SERVES 1 | 15 MINUTES

Edamame Curried Oats

INGREDIENTS

45 g (1½ oz) rolled oats

250 ml (8 fl oz) water

½ tsp curry powder

100 g (3½ oz) frozen edamame

½ tsp olive oil

salt & black pepper to taste

METHOD

- Bring the water to a boil in a small saucepan.
- Stir in oats and curry powder.
- Simmer for 5 minutes, stirring occasionally, until oats are tender and water is mostly absorbed.
- Add edamame, cover with a lid, and remove from heat. Let steam for 5 minutes.
- Stir well and serve topped with ½ tsp olive oil, salt, and black pepper.

Serving suggestion: Lime wedges

ENERGY	CARBS	PROTEIN	FAT
317 kcal (317 Cal)	35 g (1.2 oz)	15 g (0.5 oz)	13 g (0.5 oz)

SERVES 4 | 25 MINUTES

Vegan 'Smoked Salmon'

INGREDIENTS

2 large thick carrots

Marinade:

1 tbsp water

1 tbsp olive oil

2 tsp rice vinegar

1 tbsp lemon juice

¼ tsp smoked paprika

pinch of black pepper

1 tbsp olive oil

½ tsp salt

For Serving:

4 bagels, halved & toasted

8 tbsp plant-based cream cheese

4 tbsp capers

fresh dill

lemon wedges

METHOD

- Preheat the oven to 230°C (450°F). Line a baking sheet with parchment and drizzle with 1 tbsp olive oil. Slice carrots lengthwise (¼ inch or thinner).
- Arrange in a single layer and sprinkle with ½ tsp salt.
- Mix marinade ingredients thoroughly, then brush over carrots. Cover tightly with foil.
- Bake for 15 minutes. Check softness. If needed, bake for 5- minute increments until tender. Transfer hot slices to a sealed container and let cool for 1 hour to absorb flavour.
- To serve, brush bagels with any leftover marinade, spread with cream cheese, and top with carrot slices, capers, dill, and lemon wedges.

ENERGY	CARBS	PROTEIN	FAT
420 kcal (420 Cal)	63 g (2.2 oz)	15 g (0.5 oz)	12 g (0.4 oz)

SERVES 10 | 10 MINUTES

Sun-dried Tomato White Bean Dip

INGREDIENTS

300 g (10 oz) canned cannellini beans, drained & rinsed

2 cloves garlic

1 tbsp lemon juice

60 g (2 oz) sundried tomatoes, drained

2 tbsp olive oil

½ tsp salt

METHOD

- Add all ingredients to a blender or food processor.
- Blend until smooth.
- Taste and adjust seasoning if needed.

ENERGY	CARBS	PROTEIN	FAT
40 kcal (40 Cal)	8 g (0.3 oz)	2 g (0.07 oz)	0 g (0 oz)

SERVES 2 | 17 MINUTES

Chia Seed Blueberry Pancakes

INGREDIENTS

200 ml (7 fl oz) unsweetened almond milk

200 g (7 oz) self-raising flour

1 tbsp melted coconut oil

1 tsp chia seeds

3 tbsp maple syrup, divided

150 g (5 oz) blueberries

METHOD

- In a large bowl, mix flour and chia seeds. Add almond milk, melted coconut oil, and 1 tbsp maple syrup. Stir to form a smooth batter. Let rest for 5 minutes to thicken.
- Heat a little coconut oil in a pan over medium heat.
- Drop in 2 tbsp batter per pancake. Top with a few blueberries.
- Cook for 3–5 minutes until bubbles form and the underside is golden. Flip and cook for another 3–4 minutes. Serve with remaining maple syrup and blueberries.

Serving suggestion: A sprinkle of powdered sugar

ENERGY	CARBS	PROTEIN	FAT
445 kcal (445 Cal)	85 g (3.0 oz)	6 g (0.2 oz)	9 g (0.3 oz)

SERVES 12 | 30 MINUTES

Kale Quinoa Salad

INGREDIENTS

Salad:

200 g (7 oz) uncooked quinoa, rinsed

100 g (3½ oz) kale, chopped

250 g (8 oz) canned chickpeas, drained & rinsed

60 g (2 oz) red onion, finely diced

300 g (10 oz) cucumber, diced

300 g (10 oz) cherry tomatoes, halved

60 g (2 oz) croutons

½ tsp olive oil

salt & pepper to taste

Dressing:

juice & zest of 1 lemon

1 tbsp coconut sugar

1 tsp garlic powder

2 tbsp olive oil

2 tbsp apple cider vinegar,

2.75 ml (5 fl oz) water

METHOD

- Cook quinoa according to package instructions. Let cool completely.
- In a large bowl, massage kale with ½ tbsp olive oil for 1 minute until softened.
- Combine all dressing ingredients, adding salt & pepper to taste in a jar and whisk until emulsified.
- Add chickpeas, red onion, cucumber, and tomatoes to the kale.
- Add the cooled quinoa and toss well.
- Top with croutons and drizzle with dressing.

ENERGY	CARBS	PROTEIN	FAT
118 kcal (118 Cal)	20 g (0.7 oz)	5 g (0.2 oz)	2 g (0.07 oz)

SERVES 4 | 10 MINUTES

Fresh Broccoli Salad with Minty Dressing

INGREDIENTS

Dressing:

2 tsp maple syrup

1½ tsp mint, minced

1 tbsp orange juice

2 tbsp olive oil

2 tbsp apple cider vinegar

Salad:

320 g (11.3 oz) broccoli, chopped

60 g (2 oz) walnuts, chopped

40 g (1.4 oz) pumpkin seeds

60 g (2 oz) dried cranberries

METHOD

- In a small bowl, whisk together all dressing ingredients until well combined.
- In a large bowl, combine broccoli, walnuts, pumpkin seeds, and cranberries.
- Pour over the dressing and toss until evenly coated.

ENERGY	CARBS	PROTEIN	FAT
314 kcal (314 Cal)	22 g (0.8 oz)	7 g (0.2 oz)	22 g (0.8 oz)

SERVES 6 | 10 MINUTES

Vegan Chickpea 'Chicken'

INGREDIENTS

600 g (1.25 lb) chickpeas, drained & rinsed

150 g (5 oz) celery, finely chopped

125 ml (4 fl oz) vegan mayonnaise

30 g (1 oz) walnuts, chopped

juice of 1 lemon

½ tsp dried dill

¼ tsp garlic powder

¼ tsp Italian seasoning

salt & pepper to taste

METHOD

- Mash chickpeas with a fork or pulse in a food processor until flaky but not smooth.
- Add celery, mayonnaise, lemon juice, spices, and walnuts.
- Season with salt and black pepper and mix well until combined.
- Taste and adjust seasoning. Chill or serve immediately.

Serving suggestion: As a sandwich filling using Easy Homemade Bread (page 199).

ENERGY	CARBS	PROTEIN	FAT
319 kcal (319 Cal)	28 g (1.0 oz)	9 g (0.3 oz)	19 g (0.7 oz)

SERVES 6 | 25 MINUTES

Protein Pea Pasta

INGREDIENTS

500 g (1 lb) pasta of choice

500 ml (1 pt) reserved pasta water

150 g (5 oz) yellow onion, chopped

4 cloves garlic, peeled

1 tsp paprika

1 tbsp Italian seasoning

500 g (1 lb) frozen peas, thawed

375 g (12 oz) silken tofu

30 g (1 oz) fresh basil

1 tbsp olive oil

salt & pepper to taste

METHOD

- Cook pasta according to package instructions.
- Reserve 2 cups (500 ml/1 pt) of the cooking water, then set pasta aside.
- In the same pot, heat 1 tbsp olive oil over medium-high heat.
- Add onion and garlic and sauté until softened.
- Stir in paprika and Italian seasoning.
- Add peas and cook for 5 minutes, stirring often.
- Transfer mixture to a blender.
- Add tofu and basil, then blend until smooth and creamy.
- Return sauce to the pot over medium-low heat. Simmer for 5 minutes, stirring. Add pasta and toss to coat.
- Adjust consistency with reserved pasta water if needed. Season with salt and pepper.
- Garnish with red pepper flakes if desired.

ENERGY	CARBS	PROTEIN	FAT
418 kcal (418 Cal)	70 g (2.5 oz)	12 g (0.4 oz)	10 g (0.4 oz)

SERVES 4 | 25 MINUTES

Fiery Carrot & Tomato Soup

INGREDIENTS

2 tsp ginger

500 g (1 lb) carrots, peeled & chopped

750 g (1½ lb) tomatoes, chopped

1 tsp oregano

500 ml (1 pt) vegetable stock

15 g (½ oz) nutritional yeast

basil leaves, sliced, to garnish

2 tbsp olive oil

1 tsp salt

METHOD

- In a large pot, heat 2 tbsp olive oil over medium heat.
- Add ginger and carrots, and sauté for 1 minute.
- Add tomatoes, oregano, and 1 tsp salt. Stir.
- Pour in vegetable stock and add nutritional yeast.
- Bring to a boil.
- Reduce heat, cover, and simmer for 20–25 minutes until carrots are tender.
- Blend until smooth. Taste and adjust seasoning.
- Garnish with sliced basil and serve hot.

ENERGY	CARBS	PROTEIN	FAT
172 kcal (172 Cal)	20 g (0.7 oz)	5 g (0.2 oz)	8 g (0.3 oz)

SERVES 1 | 45 MINUTES

Roasted Cabbage & Crispy Chickpeas

INGREDIENTS

Veggies:

200 g (7 oz) white cabbage, thinly sliced

45 g (1½ oz) kale, stems removed & chopped

30 g (1 oz) pumpkin seeds

1 tsp olive oil

salt & pepper to taste

Chickpeas:

200 g (7 oz) chickpeas, drained & rinsed

1 tsp smoked paprika

1 tsp garlic granules

1 tsp olive oil

salt & pepper to taste

Dressing:

1 lemon, sliced (skin on)

1 clove garlic, finely chopped

1 tbsp maple syrup

1 tsp Dijon mustard

1 tsp olive oil

salt & pepper to taste

METHOD

- Preheat the oven to 200°C (390°F). Toss chickpeas with paprika, garlic granules, 1 tsp olive oil, salt, and pepper.
- Spread on a baking tray and bake for 30–35 minutes, shaking occasionally, until crispy.
- On a separate tray, toss cabbage with 1 tsp olive oil, salt, and pepper. Roast for 10–15 minutes.
- Add pumpkin seeds and kale. Toss well, then roast for a further 10 minutes.
- Heat 1 tsp olive oil in a pan. Sear lemon slices for 2 minutes on each side.
- Blend seared lemons with garlic, maple syrup, mustard, 1 tbsp olive oil, salt, and pepper until creamy.
- Toss dressing through the roasted vegetables.
- Top with crispy chickpeas and serve warm.

ENERGY	CARBS	PROTEIN	FAT
464 kcal (464 Cal)	46 g (1.6 oz)	16 g (0.6 oz)	24 g (0.8 oz)

SERVES 3 | 20 MINUTES

Tofu Red Curry Noodles

INGREDIENTS

150 g (5 oz) dry ramen noodles

2 tbsp sesame oil, divided

250 g (8 oz) firm tofu, cut into cubes

1 clove garlic, chopped

1 tbsp fresh ginger, chopped

1 tbsp Thai red curry paste

2 tsp tomato paste

250 ml (8 fl oz) canned coconut milk

juice of ½ lime

2 tsp tamari

2 green onions, sliced

METHOD

- Cook ramen noodles until al dente. Drain and set aside.
- Heat 1 tbsp sesame oil in a pan over medium-high heat. Add tofu and cook for 6–8 minutes until golden brown on all sides.
- Remove from the pan and set aside.
- Add remaining oil to the same pan. Sauté garlic and ginger for 30 seconds. Stir in curry paste and tomato paste. Cook for 1 minute.
- Pour in coconut milk and bring to a gentle boil. Reduce heat and simmer for 2–3 minutes. Stir in lime juice and tamari.
- Add noodles and tofu.
- Toss to coat in the sauce.
- Stir in green onions and serve hot.

ENERGY	CARBS	PROTEIN	FAT
372 kcal (372 Cal)	44 g (1.6 oz)	13 g (0.5 oz)	16 g (0.6 oz)

SERVES 12 SLICES | 45 MINUTES

Easy Homemade Bread

INGREDIENTS

500 g (1 lb) all-purpose flour

60 g (2 oz) coconut sugar

2¼ tsp instant yeast

375 ml (12 fl oz) water

1 tsp salt

METHOD

- In a large bowl, whisk together flour, sugar, yeast, and 1 tsp salt.
- Add water and stir until a rough dough forms.
- Turn out onto a floured surface and knead briefly.
- Shape into a ball.
- Place dough into a greased bowl, cover, and let rise in a warm place for 60–90 minutes until doubled in size.
- Knead a few times then shape the dough into a loaf and place in a parchment-lined loaf pan.
- Let rise again until it peaks over the top, about 60–90 minutes. This depends on the temperature in the room - the warmer the room, the faster the rise.
- Make a shallow slash along the top.
- Bake at 190°C (375°F) for 30–35 minutes.
- Cool completely before slicing.

ENERGY	CARBS	PROTEIN	FAT
136 kcal (136 Cal)	32 g (1.1 oz)	2 g (0.07 oz)	0 g (0 oz)

SERVES 2 | 5 MINUTES

Chocolate Chia Flax Seed Pudding

INGREDIENTS

250 ml (8 fl oz) oat milk

1 tbsp cocoa powder

¼ tsp stevia powder

45 g (1½ oz) chia seeds

15 g (½ oz) ground flaxseed (linseed)

45 g (1½ oz) blueberries

METHOD

- Add all ingredients except blueberries to a jar. Shake or stir until fully combined.
- Refrigerate for at least 3 hours or overnight, until thickened.
- Stir well before serving.
- Divide into bowls and top with blueberries.

Tip: Add vegan protein powder to up the protein content.

ENERGY	CARBS	PROTEIN	FAT
198 kcal (198 Cal)	21 g (0.7 oz)	6 g (0.2 oz)	10 g (0.4 oz)

SERVES 9 | 35 MINUTES

Tahini Walnut Blondies

INGREDIENTS

2 bananas

125 g (4 oz) tahini

60 ml (2 fl oz) oat milk

75 g (2½ oz) walnuts, chopped

15 g (½ oz) sesame seeds

100 g (3½ oz) maple syrup

60 g (2 oz) coconut sugar

1 tsp vanilla extract

¾ tsp baking powder

¼ tsp baking soda (bicarbonate of soda)

150 g (5 oz) all-purpose flour

¼ tsp salt

METHOD

- Preheat the oven to 170°C (340°F). Line a square 20×20 cm (8×8 inch) baking pan with parchment paper.
- In a bowl, mash bananas until smooth. Whisk in tahini, oat milk, maple syrup, coconut sugar, and vanilla extract.
- In a separate bowl, mix flour, baking powder, baking soda, and ¼ tsp salt.
- Fold dry mixture into wet ingredients until fully incorporated.
- Stir in walnuts.
- Pour batter into the prepared pan. Smooth the top and sprinkle with sesame seeds.
- Bake for 20–25 minutes, until golden and set. Let it cool before slicing.

Tip: Add vegan protein powder to up the protein content.

ENERGY	CARBS	PROTEIN	FAT
229 kcal (229 Cal)	24 g (0.8 oz)	4 g (0.1 oz)	13 g (0.5 oz)

SERVES 2 | 5 MINUTES

Anti-Inflammatory Tropical Protein Shake

INGREDIENTS

200 g (7 oz) frozen pineapple

200 g (7 oz) frozen mango

250 ml (8 fl oz) oat milk

100 ml (3 fl oz) coconut water

30 g (1 oz) unsweetened shredded coconut

45 g (1½ oz) unsalted cashews, roasted

1 medjool date

½ inch fresh ginger, grated

½ tsp turmeric powder

¼ tsp black pepper

METHOD

- Add all ingredients plus to a high-powered blender.
- Blend until smooth, scraping down the sides as needed.
- Serve immediately.

Tip: Add vegan protein powder to up the protein content.

ENERGY	CARBS	PROTEIN	FAT
416 kcal (416 Cal)	52 g (1.8 oz)	7 g (0.2 oz)	20 g (0.7 oz)

RECIPE INDEX

First published in 2025 by New Holland Publishers
newhollandpublishers.com

A record of this book is held at the National Library of Australia.

ISBN 9781760798475

Managing Director: Fiona Schultz
General Manager/Publisher: Olga Dementiev
Project Editor: Xavier Waterkeyn
Designer: Andrew Davies
Production Director: Arlene Gippert

Keep up with New Holland Publishers:
NewHollandPublishers
@newhollandpublishers